"The Adventures of

SASSY

the Red Hat Mascot"

Rose Olson

Hope you giggle at least once!

Rose

"The Adventures of Sassy the Red Hat Mascot"

Tellwell Talent
www.tellwell.ca

ISBN
978-0-2288-0726-1 (Paperback)
978-0-2288-0727-8 (eBook)

This book is dedicated to

THE SASSY R.E.D.'s (Real Elegant Dames)
A RED HAT SOCIETY GROUP
IN PEACE RIVER, ALBERTA, CANADA

with special thanks to

Jan Klaus, founding Queen
who said to me at the
15 year reunion
"Why don't you write a book about Sassy's adventures"
So, I did....

THANK YOU

Jan
Debra
Betty
Sharon
Wendy

A SPECIAL HUG FOR

Tariq
Jason

AND LOTS OF LOVE FOR
MY HUSBAND

Burt

I could not have finished this book
without help from
ALL OF YOU!

Rose

FOREWORD

My husband Burt and I moved from the little community of Kitchener in British Columbia to Peace River, Alberta in February 2001. While Burt was working at Home Hardware, he was introduced to Judy who trained him to work on the till.

We became friends and in the fall of 2002 I was invited to a supper with a group of ladies 50+ years old. This club was the Sassy REDs (Real Elegant Dames), a registered group of the Red Hat Society, which was started by Sue Ellen Cooper in the United States. If you wish learn more or to join this great organization, log on to: www.redhatsociety.com.

`There were a lot of ladies at this supper. Each of us had something wrong with our meal. I had blue (rotten) cauliflower. At the end of the meal, Judy dug out a pen and piece of paper from her purse and started writing a list of things that were wrong. The note said that because of these things, we were not going to leave a tip for their services.

I nodded and silently agreed and then said, "Yes, I definitely want to join this fantastic group!"

About a year and a half later, Burt and I went to a yard sale and found this adorable, stuffed purple toy dog.

And the rest, so they say, is history…

Dear readers: my wish is that you giggle twice and laugh three times while reading this novel because believe it not, these things really did happen!

As told through Sassy's eyes of course.

Rose

Chapter 1

I am a stuffed toy dog about twenty-four inches, or sixty centimeters, high with my ears down and about thirty inches, or seventy-six centimeters, high with my ears straight up, and I weigh about four pounds, or ten kilograms. I am bright purple with fluffy silver and white ears, feet, and a cute little tail. I have a big, puffy black nose and a smile. There is a black collar around my neck with a little sliver heart attached to it.

My eyes—well, my eyes are what make me unique. They are medium-sized white ovals with little black dots that are close together with one pointed upward and the other downward. It makes it a little difficult to see correctly, but I manage.

I was sitting on a yard sale table in the town of Peace River, Alberta, Canada, with a couple of stuffed toy friends when a blonde-haired lady and her husband arrived. She came over, looked at me and smiled. She said that I was cute. Cute! Me? Cute? She picked me up, really looked me over and then put me back down.

She walked around a while, looking at other items and then came back and looked at me again. I smiled at her. She started to giggle. I thought that I must be getting to her. She picked me up and took me to my owner. She asked how much I was worth. What is worth? Is it a cost, price or what? I heard her offer some money for me. My owner accepted. I had no idea what was happening but I knew my life would never be the same. And boy was I right.

Here is my story.

As we were walking away from the table, the blonde lady's husband asked her why she was "buying" me. She said something about my beautiful ears, feet and tail. She also said something about a group of ladies that she was involved with that wear red hats and purple clothes.

"Hey! I am purple. Now all I need is a red hat, huh?" I said.

This lady giggled again and cuddled me. I think she loves me! She carried me to a sort of brownish, square, metal thing. It had four round black things on the bottom. She opened a door near the back of this big metal object and then placed me on a bench of some sort. She shut the door and then she and her husband each opened a door, got in and sat down on a padded seat. They were talking quietly. They each pulled something over their shoulder and I heard two clicking sounds. He called her Rose; she called him Burt.

I asked, "Who are you people, and where are you taking me?"

No answer. Maybe they do not hear me or they do not understand me. They were still just talking quietly to each other. I heard a hum and then we started to move. He had his hands on this medium-sized wheel and was steering around several sharp corners, and I almost fell over. I travelled to a lot of places that day. They kept pointing at funny little signs on the side of the road and then stopping, getting out of the moving brownish thing and coming back. Sometimes they brought things back with them and put those items in the back, which they called a trunk. They told me they were having a fun day going to yard sales. They said they enjoy doing this when they both have the day off work. What is work?

After a lot of travelling around the town, going up and down the streets and up and down hills, the brownish square thing finally stopped. They gathered up everything they bought and Rose picked me up and carried me into a big white building. They went up a bunch of stairs and down a hallway to a door.

Rose kept looking at me and giggled again. She said that I was cute and that I was "getting to her." She mumbled something about my eyes. Of course it had to be my eyes.

She took a key, opened the door and then took me inside to a square room and put me on a little chair. I sat there for some time while she was arranging and putting away the new items she purchased. I did not mind because the little chair was soft and comfortable. I also happened to see a grey and white animal with big green eyes looking at me as he walked into the kitchen. Rose finally came back, really looked at me again and twitched my ears. She made one go up and the other go down. It tickled.

She said, "I know what I am going to do to you," and then she left the room.

I wondered what she was up to when she arrived with two little pieces of bright purple ribbon. She tied them on to the bottom of my ears. She picked me up and took me to a little room that had a funny looking type of shiny glass that she called a mirror. When I looked up, I could see myself and the ribbon on my ears. I liked that, it looked good and gave me a bit of pizzazz. Yep, I liked this lady.

Rose and Burt kept leaving me alone for long periods of time. I heard them talking about why this was happening. It was because both of them have full time jobs. She works in a bakery and he works at a Hardware Store. They sure are gone a lot. They do not leave or come back at the same time.

"Help, Help! Somebody help me!" I shouted.

I kept seeing the grey and white fuzzy animal with big white teeth and green eyes looking at me. He took his paw, (thank goodness there are no claws) and whacked me on my cheek, almost knocking me off my chair before trying to bite my feet and ears. I heard Rose telling him to leave me alone, but he won't do as she says. He is a cat and his name is Casper. He sure is big, but I am bigger than he is, so maybe that is why he attacks me. I have seen other stuffed toys that he does not bother, but I am new here and the silver in my hair is real shiny and that is what he is attracted to. No one is around when he whacks me so I guess it is up to me to try and become friends with this savage beast.

I heard Rose talking on the telephone to someone about bringing me for a little visit. I would be a surprise for this lady. I saw her as she brought this big white thing over to me, opened it up, and then picked me up and tried to put me into it. It was soft and pliable. Hey, I have company.

"Hi there, little brown fuzzy friend and little red buddy." I said. "Hey, Fuzzy, I like your hat and little jacket."

They told me that they were both teddy bears. They said that they did not have names yet and asked what my name was.

"No, I do not have a name yet either, but I heard the name "Sassy" mentioned for me," I replied.

"Do you know where are we going?" Red Buddy asked.

"I heard her talking to a friend about a visit," I replied.

Rose finally squeezed me into this soft thing and then closed the top really tight so that there was very little air left for the three of us to breathe.

"Oh my, I think I am going to faint. Help! Help! I can't breathe. Rose, help!" I screamed.

Oh good, she heard me. She opened it and pulled me up by my ears so that my ears and head were sticking out.

"Thank you. I can breathe better now," I said.

Whew, that was scary for a bit. There was enough fresh air for the two teddies now too.

Rose took me to that brown thing with the four round rubber things on the bottom again. I know what it is now. It is called a car. She opened the door and put the thing with me in it on the seat right next to her then went around and opened the other door and got in. She sat down, put this strap-like thing over her shoulder and I heard a clicking sound. I heard that sound before. Rose put a small metal thing into a little hole beside the steering wheel. There was a strange humming noise and then she moved this funny looking handle and away we started to move.

I wondered where we were going now. I watched as she drove around a bunch of corners and stopped a couple of times and then started again. She said that those red things on the side of the road were stop signs. There was also a special hanging light in the middle of the street that turned from green to yellow to red. I did not see these things before because I was sitting in the back seat. What a difference riding in the front seat made. We finally stopped at a brown building. Rose told me she had to hide me again, so she tucked my head and ears back in the white thing. She said I was going to be a surprise for this lady and picked up the thing that my new friends and I were in, went to the door and rang the bell.

I heard her talking to the lady.

"What's in the plastic bag?" the lady asked.

Rose followed the lady into the kitchen and then took me out of the plastic bag and put me on a big table. This new lady started to giggle. Rose introduced me to Judy.

"Hi, Judy," I said.

Nope, I do not do last names. It is too complicated and too much to memorize.

Judy said that I look real elegant and sassy. Maybe it was my bright purple colour, cool eyes or my fluffy ears, feet and tail. Maybe I was the "total package."

Rose and Judy were talking about me being a mascot for the Sassy REDs. That stands for "Real Elegant Dames." This group belongs to the Red Hat Society. It was the first one started in northern Alberta in 2002 and their Chapter number is 4956. The Red Hat Society was originally founded in the United States by Sue Ellen Cooper. The ladies from Peace River get together about once a month or so just to go out and have fun. The ladies that are over fifty years old wear red hats and purple outfits. What an odd combination of colours! The ladies that are not quite fifty yet wear pink hats and lavender outfits until they "reduate"—which means they graduate to red and purple.

Elegant! Elegant! Judy kept saying that I am elegant. Elegant is part of their name. Oh, I like these ladies. Judy picked me up, really looked me over, set me back down and then said that I looked in good shape.

"Of course I am in good shape," I said. "I do exercise—at least uh, well, about an hour a day. I am a little behind by about—uh, well, about a year," I stammered.

Rose asked Judy if I would be a good candidate for the Sassy RED's mascot.

"What is a mascot?" I asked.

No answer. I do not think they can understand me yet.

They are talking about different things that I can do with the girls : attending coffees, visiting other groups, visiting other ladies, going to house parties and having fun with whatever the ladies do.

After a lot of conversation between these two ladies, they finally agreed that I would be their mascot.

"What is a mascot? Is it something good?" I asked again.

No answer, but they both looked at me when I asked that question. Hmmm, maybe they are starting to hear me.

Rose was explaining to Judy about an organization that she was with that had a green frog for a mascot, and that a story was kept of the trips and meetings. Judy loved the idea and Rose explained that she had done a lot of this type of writing and would love to keep a running diary of whatever happened. It sure sounded like I could be real busy. I hope so because I want to have some fun. They want to call me Sassy. That's cool. I can handle Sassy.

I heard a funny ding dong noise; it is a door bell. Judy got up and went to see who was there. In came another member of the Sassy REDs who came for a talk. Judy and Rose introduced me to Christine. Her eyes lit up when she saw me. She giggled, said that I looked adorable and then hugged me. She loved the idea of me being their mascot. The three ladies then talked about ideas for a Christmas tree and looked at a bunch of pictures.

"What is a Christmas tree? What are pictures?" I asked.

No answer, but they showed me some pictures of what a Christmas tree looks like. I think it is working. I think they start to understand me. The tree had a lot of twinkly lights and round balls on it and even a big shiny star on the top. It was a long meeting, and then Rose and Christine went back home. Judy wanted me to stay with her for a while. That is good because then I don't have to fight with Casper.

Judy took me to a little room that had a soft rectangular piece of furniture called a couch. I sat with a bunch of teddy bears of all different colours and sizes. My other two friends that Rose had in that plastic bag with me are here too. They said that they are all going to be a special project. The teddy bears are telling me that they will be connected to a big green thing called a Christmas tree that will have little flashing lights. The red teddy bear will be dressed up like an angel and sit on the top of the tree. What is an angel? It sounds heavenly. The tree will be at the Festival of Trees, which is an annual gala held in the town of Peace River every November. There are many trees as well as other Christmas related items for residents to bid on. The money collected will go to a special organization to help women in need. What is money?

I stayed with Judy for a couple of days. I heard the doorbell chime, and in came another Red Hat lady. I heard her walking with Judy to the room I was sitting in. Judy introduced me to Joyce.

"Hi, Joyce, I'm Sassy," I said.

She looked at me, smiled and then told me that I looked elegant. There is that famous word again. I like that word—elegant. She said that she loved my silvery ears.

"What about my cute eyes? Do you like them too?" I asked.

I liked her. Judy and Joyce were wondering where Rose found me and how much she paid for me, but Rose kept insisting that I am her little secret.

Then Rose came back.

"Do you like my red hat that I borrowed from one of my teddy bear friends? Hey ladies, when will I get my own hat?" I asked.

Oh wow, Rose found a hat for me. She said it is a baseball cap. It has a white elastic string to go under my chin. What is a chin? I did not think that will work for me, but Judy tried to put the elastic string around my ears.

"Ouch. That hurts. Hey, Judy, that is not going to work!" I said.

She looked at me kind of funny and then she finally quit trying to put that little hat on me. She said that the hat would fit but it may need some "poofing." I think that is the word she used. What's poofing? Will poofing hurt my head?

"It is a cute hat. I can use it to go golfing, have a picnic in the park or go for a jog," I said. "A jog—that is strenuous exercise. Forget that I said that, okay?" I exclaimed.

Rose returned later with the poofed hat. It fit but it sure was stiff though. I wondered what she did to it. I could use this hat for a casual outing.

Later I heard Judy talking about a concert that she and some other ladies are planning to attend.

She was all dressed up in a purple outfit and a pretty red hat as she walked by the room I was sitting in with my teddy bear friends.

"Judy," I called out to her. She stopped and peeked in the door.

"Can I go, can I? Huh? Can I go to the concert?" I asked.

No answer. She put up her hand.

"Please. I would love to go see some people on stage singing and dancing," I said.

Nope, still no answer but now she shook her head. She walked away to the main door. I could hear her footsteps.

"Judy! Judy!!!!! Can't you hear me?" I yelled. "JUDY!!" I yelled as loud as I could.

Nope, she couldn't hear me. I heard the door close. She had gone to the concert without me. I am kind of new to these ladies so maybe she just forgot about me. I will ask her about it when she gets back.

Judy and eight other Red Hatters went to the Women's Shelter Benefit Concert. There was great talent and beautiful costumes and dancers. The crowd participated with young George and his "Yellow Submarine" song. There were four good-looking men doing the "Hambones." There were also the Croaking Four which consisted of three men and one lady. The Scottish Dancers and the Mizurka Dancers also performed.

Judy got home, came into the room and talked to me about the concert. She said that it was a full house. They did not have a seat for me and the cost would have been ten dollars. So THAT is why she did not take me. Is that a lot of money?

Rose came back with more hats for me. She said that she would paint them red and put some flowers on them. She tried them on my head to make sure they would fit. Yep, they did. Wow, now that I have some hats, all I needed was someplace to wear them.

Sometime later she returned, and she brought my new hats. They looked great. They have such a different variety of pretty flowers on them. She hot glued them on so that they will not fall off. I am going home with her. She put one of the hats on my head and then took this big sharp pointy thing and stabbed it in into my head.

"Ouch, that hurts." I said.

"Sorry, it is a stick pin," she said. "I am doing it so the hat will not fall off your head."

Good plan, but it still hurts. Maybe Scotch taping it on would be easier and not as painful.

We drove back to her place and she put me back on that soft little chair.

Rose and Burt were both at work when I heard a knock on the door.

"Come in," I said.

There was another knock on the door.

"Who is there?" I asked.

It's me, Judy," she said. "Is anyone home?"

I recognised her voice. "Yes, it's me, Sassy," I yelled so she could hear me.

The door was locked, so she could not get in the apartment. I found out later that several Red Hat ladies made a quick decision to go to the Athabasca Hall to see the Sharon Krueshel musical. Judy had stopped in at Rose's place to let her know. The girls each had a salad at McDonald's and then went to the event. It was a full house like last time. Okay, I understand. There was that cost to get in too. I guess that I have to be satisfied that I cannot go to anything that costs lots of money.

Rose planned a "Christmas in July" luncheon party at her place. She decorated her apartment with trees and lots of snowmen. She had been making little gifts and working on games to play too.

I heard knocking on the door. The ladies must be coming. Rose opened the door, let them in, and they each brought a wrapped package that they put under the tree. Rose introduced me to all the ladies and explained to them that I was their new mascot. They all loved the idea and looked upon me as the newest member of their Red Hat group. Rose gave each lady a little, purple dress fridge magnet that she made. She put a bunch of different hats on me and Christine took pictures. Boy have I ever got a lot of dots in front of my eyes.

The girls were told to bring a decorated hat to be judged in a contest. Joyce was the winner; her hat was a box wrapped like a Christmas gift. What a great idea. Hey, my Santa hat was not on the table for judging. It was probably too small and no one would have seen it amongst the other hats.

The ladies played a game with a broom. Rose is saying "We are all having a great time," and is bouncing the broom up and down at the same time. The other ladies try to say and do everything that Rose does—but they are missing a little something. They are not quite getting it right. Ah ha! That's what they forgot—the "ahem" to clear their throats right at the beginning of the sentence.

For the second game, Rose handed the girls a ball of wool and scissors, and then said that the girls had to cut a piece of wool.

"What size?" they all asked.

Rose shrugged she shoulders and said, "Cut what you will need."

Judy won. She cut her piece to fit around her ankle.

The third game was about memory. Rose had fifty little items on a tray that she passed around to let everyone see. She said that memory is the "second" thing to go with age—the waistline is first. What's memory? My waistline is just fine. It has not changed, even with all the goodies I eat now. Judy and Christine tied with remembering fourteen items, so they each won a prize. Sally won the door prize.

Each lady chose a gift from under the tree and then opened it. There was a lot of paper and boxes all over the floor. Everyone was so excited. Someone said that it "looks like Christmas." So, *this* is Christmas, huh? It's a time of fun and gift giving.

Luncheon was a veggie platter, salmon and egg salad buns, meats, cheeses, and shrimp. Rose also baked and decorated a cake shaped like a Red Hat lady. There was punch to drink.

Christine presented Rose with a gift of a little angel for hosting the party.

After lunch, the ladies were talking about maybe hosting a convention. What's a convention? Is it something fun? A camp-out sounded like a good idea too because then the ladies would not have to worry about booking motels and a hall. What's a motel?

The girls were also discussing title names for everyone. Something royal, like court jester, duchess, baroness and countess.

"Hey, what title can I have?" I asked.

I know that I am a mascot, but I would love have a title too. I will think of something and then bring it up to the girls the next time they are together. Hmm, what can my title be?

Goodbye, ladies; see you next time. This was sure a fun afternoon. Rose said that she wanted to do this again next year.

I wonder what the next event will be. Maybe a couple of the ladies will go out for a coffee and invite me. Joyce wants to have a tea party, and Judy wants to plan a backyard bonfire. Sounds like fun. I sure hope that I can go.

CHAPTER 2

Rose told me that I will be going to a special tea. She put on one of my hats and stuck pins in my ears so that my hat would not fall off. It didn't hurt as much as the last time she did it. I must be getting used to it. It worked though because the hat stayed on. She explained that she could not go to the tea because she had to work. She does packaging and cake decorating at the bakery.

Christine arrived and was talking to Rose about the tea party. She picked me up and carried me to a silvery-brown car. I recognize cars now. They sure come in a lot of different shapes and colours. She opened the door, and then put me in the back seat and put something around me so that I could not move.

"What are you doing?" I asked Christine.

"It is a seat belt," she said. "It will protect you." She said that there is a law about wearing seat belts.

"What is a law? I asked.

Christine explained that if I don't wear a seat belt and the police stop us, I could be fined a lot of money.

"It sure is confining, but I do feel safe," I said.

I remembered Rose putting the seat belt on when she took me to see Judy. Christine said that she had some errands to do. What are errands? She parked, opened the door, got out of the car, went into a store and then came back. She did this a lot of times. Finally, she told me that she was done and we would be going to her home now. We travelled through the town and then headed up this big hill. We went over a big steel holey thing that had flowing water under it. She explained that it was a bridge and the river was called Peace River. We travelled for a long way. I wondered why we had slowed down. It was because she turned off the paved highway and onto a bumpy road. She said that it is called a gravel road; it is not smooth like the pavement. I was moving up and down on the seat. We went up and then down a big hill. My tummy did a flip flop and I did some moving. Yes, its's a good thing that I had my seat belt on because I would have ended up on the floor several times. Then I could see a big house. I knew it must be her place. She stopped, took off my seat belt and carried me into her house. Wow, nice place. She put me on a comfy chair.

Hey, she has one of those four-legged purring, fuzzy animals that Rose has. This cat is black and white, and I can see big claws on his front feet. I sure hope it will not attack me like Casper does.

Christine's family showed up and when she introduced me to them, they looked at me kind of funny. I guess they do not understand about me yet or else it is my eyes. She explained that I am going to a special tea with her and a few other Red Hat ladies tomorrow. Now they really looked at her kind of funny. I bet they were wondering who would really take a stuffed purple dog with weird eyes to a tea party. Only the Sassy REDs of course! She went into another room, and when she returned she had her camera with her and took a bunch of pictures of me. She said that the ones from the Christmas in July party did not turn out good. I have those spots in front of my eyes again.

It sure is quiet here. No car noises because I am in the country and the air smells nice and fresh. The trees are swaying back and forth from a breeze. I better get to sleep early because I have a big day tomorrow. This will be my first official out-of-town outing. I am so excited. No worries about money with this one. I shut my eyes.

I had a good night's sleep and now I am raring to go. I was introduced to Heather, another Red Hat lady. She said that I am gorgeous. Ooh, I think I blushed and turned from purple to red. We all went outside, and then I was put on the back seat of Heather's big car, called a van, and of course had the seat belt put around me. Judy is here too. Everyone giggled about me being buckled in. Normal stuffed toys never have such things happen to them.

We travelled back to the pavement and then on to the main highway. We drove for a long time. I have never travelled this far before. We even drove through a little town called Grimshaw and another town called Fairview. The girls are all excited and talked about other ideas for getting together. Wow, look at all the trees and big open fields. There are lots of corners and a great big hill to go down. We finally got to a place called Dunvegan Gardens. What a beautiful place. There are lots of flowers, trees and walking paths. We all met in a big building. Look at all those tables and chairs.

The ladies sat me on one of the chairs. My eyes just peeked over the table.

"This is not going to work, girls. I cannot see anything. I will need a higher chair or else sit me right on the top of the table," I said.

They must have heard me because Judy looked at me kind of funny, giggled and then came over and picked me up and set me on the end of the long table. Now I can see everyone just fine.

Pauline owns the gardens and was the hostess for the day. There are sweet treats for munching as well as tea and coffee.

Everyone put their name on a little piece of paper and placed it in a big bowl. That was for a door prize. When the draw was done, Christine's name was pulled. She was so excited to be the winner. The prize was a huge basket filled with a candle, teas, smelly soaps, writing cards and even a small red purse.

There are a lot of ladies at this function. The girls were talking about the Red Hat Society and all the fun they have. They wondered if anyone here would like to start a new chapter.

Our group could give them a lot of advice. At this time though, no one seemed to be interested.

Then it was time to leave. We said our goodbyes and were invited back next month to a Christmas open house. Several ladies said they would love to come back.

"Can I come too? I asked. I had a great time today and would love to see everyone again. Can I?" I asked again.

No one said anything. If Rose is working and cannot come, I hope I can get a ride with someone. We all had a great time visiting and promoting the Red Hat Society. We all got hugs and then walked back to the van. The girls buckled me into the back seat again, and we headed back to Peace River. Christine still wanted me to visit with her, so when Heather drove her home, I got out with her. After I stayed with Christine for a nice long visit, she took me back to Rose's place.

Rose told me that Judy is calling a special meeting to discuss plans for the next couple of months. I was told that I will be staying with Judy after the meeting because the girls and I will be going to Dunvegan again in a couple of days. Rose has to work again and cannot go. She pinned one of my favourite hats to my ears again. Hey, I felt a little poke but it did not hurt this time. I sure am excited about this meeting. Rose carried me to her car and buckled me in the back seat. Her husband, Burt, is going to drive us to Judy's place. He said something about her being "weird" because she put a seat belt around me.

"Hey, I need to be protected too, don't I? I asked.

Rose explained to her husband that all the girls are doing this to Sassy now. Burt just smiled, shook his head and then he drove us to Judy's place. Rose opened the back door of the car, unbuckled me and carried me to Judy's house and rang the doorbell.

She walked in and I looked around and said, "There are lots of ladies here for this special meeting."

Rose said, "There is someone special I want you to meet."

She carried me to a lady with dark hair and introduced me to Jan. I FINALLY GET TO MEET JAN!! She is the lady who started the Sassy REDs group, making her our founding Queen. She fell in love with me instantly, and I fell in love with her. She loved my fuzzy ears and feet and especially my eyes. She giggled, gave me a great big hug and welcomed me as the newest member of the Sassy REDs. I felt so proud. She said that she had heard about me but seeing me was something totally different. I even got my picture taken with her.

Founding Queen Jan and Sassy

I met some more new ladies; one of them even tickled my tail and then giggled. She asked Rose where I came from. Again she would not tell, saying that it was her little secret.

Judy put a shiny, round thing into a machine that played music. She called it a CD. It was a special song about Red Hatters. All the ladies stood up, twisted, turned and wiggled. It is called dancing. I even danced with everyone. Hey, this is fun.

Judy had some red boas for sale that she bought in Edmonton. What's Edmonton?

I asked, "Hey, ladies, can I have a boa too? Huh? There are some little ones that would look good on me."

There are red sequined and white gloves for sale too. I cannot wear that kind of glove because my paws are too big.

Judy must have heard me because she looked at all the boas, picked up a little one, came over to me and put one around my neck. It fit perfectly.

"Thank you so much, Judy," I said.

The girls talked about decorating the Christmas tree with teddy bears for the Festival of Trees in November. I met most of the teddy bears the last time I visited Judy. They sounded excited. The girls decided that we were all going to go to Christine's for a work bee. I hope that I can go too. I have been to her house before.

The ladies finalized the plans for the next couple of months: Two girls planned a dinner and movie night sometime in the month of September; an orange night was being planned in October for Halloween. Hmm, I need to wear something orange, huh? There are plans for an Elvis night in January. Who is Elvis? Why is he called the King? Jan and Judy are planning a Hawaiian night in January too. What's Hawaii? Christine is planning to go there for a holiday. What's a holiday? What's a muumuu? Sounds like a cow of some sort. It sure looks like a busy couple of months ahead. I will have to make plans to attend all these events.

Instead of meeting just once month, the girls want to meet for a coffee night the first Wednesday and third Thursday of each month at Travellers Hotel restaurant.

The ladies also started to talk about a trip to Las Vegas to attend a Red Hat convention!

"What's a convention?" I asked.

No answer. I do not think they hear me. I will just listen and find out more information. It sounds like it is a long way away. Several girls are talking about wanting to go. I wonder if they will take me. They said that it is in the United States, and that is a big country way down south of Peace River.

We would have to travel by car to an airport, fly in a big airplane, get to a hotel and then finally find our way to the convention. We would meet a bunch of other Red Hat ladies, have fun, go back to the hotel, fly in the airplane again and finally drive back home. That would take a long time too.

"Are dogs allowed?" I asked.

Judy said, "Dogs need to have their shots in order to travel to another country."

"Shots? SHOTS! That will hurt. I do not like shots!" I replied.

The ladies said that passports are needed too.

"What are passports?" I questioned.

I learned that it is complicated to get a passport. It takes time and money. Then I heard them say that it would be easier if they just shoved me into a suitcase and then sneaked me on board the plane that way. I would end up being in the cargo bay with all the rest of the luggage. Sometimes luggage gets tossed around so I might end up with bruises. Oh boy, that sure sounds real scary being squished into a suitcase and being banged around at the airport. They then mentioned something about luggage getting lost. This does not sound like fun to me.

The ladies are whispering now, saying that it would be easier to get me through customs if I was in a suitcase.

"What is customs?" I asked.

They looked at me and then looked away and started whispering a lot so that I could not hear everything they said. This trip sounds real complicated. The ladies said something about the high cost to travel in an airplane and get tickets for the convention. There is that cost thing again. I really do not think I will be going. I am sure that you girls will check all this out and let me know what you find out.

Goodbye, ladies. It was a real good meeting. Sure is quiet now. It's a good thing that Judy put me back on the couch with the other teddy bears because I heard an odd yipping noise. I guess I will find out some day what that is. Now I just have to wait for that trip to Dunvegan again.

It sure had been a busy day, and I am tired; I decided to take a little nap, so I closed my eyes. Car ride, convention, airplane, stuffed in a suitcase, bumps and bruises, all those ladies having fun, heading back to Peace River…

"What happened?" I asked the teddy bears next to me.

They said that I was moving back and forth and moaning and giggling. It seemed so real. It must have been a dream because I have not gone anywhere.

The next time I see Judy, she is running around getting ready for our special day trip. We are going back to Dunvegan Gardens for a Christmas tea party. She is all dressed up in a nice purple outfit. She mumbles something about the weather and looks worried. I heard her complain and grumble about snow. What is snow? I just looked outside and saw stuff falling from the sky. It looks like rain. She is packing up her pretty hat and other things and putting them in plastic bags so they will not get wet. Finally, Judy put a beautiful, red hat and my little red boa on me. Ooh, I feel real special.

Judy is looking at me real funny and shaking her head. She went into the kitchen and then came back. She had some big black plastic bags in her hands.

"Hey, what are you doing? Judy. JUDY! Talk to me. Tell me what is happening," I said to her.

"Sorry, Sassy, but I have to do this," she said.

She picked me up and stuffed me in a big black plastic bag. Actually, it was two big bags. I have trouble breathing in them.

"Help! Help me!" I screamed.

Oh good, she heard me. Judy opened the bag, looked at me and then said, "I am putting you in the bags because it is pouring rain outside and I do not want you to get wet."

"Okay, I understand," I said.

She tied the bag back up again and I waited. It sure is dark in here and stuffy too. She finally picked up the bag with her hat and the bags with me in them and walked outside. Boy was she right. There is a lot of rain hitting the plastic bag that she stuffed me in. She went running to her car, opened the trunk and squished me into a tight corner.

"Sorry, Sassy, but there are just too many ladies and parcels, so there is no room for you to sit on the back seat and be buckled in like you normally are," she said.

"Can I sit on someone's lap?" I asked.

"It is against the law not to wear a seat belt, and I not want to take any chances being stopped by the police," she replied.

I guess I have to be satisfied to stay in these bags.

"Hey, Judy, how long will I be in here?" I asked.

Nope, too late, she shut the trunk and did not hear me. I heard her open the door, get in and start up the car. She drove real slow around town and picked up the rest of the girls. They all sounded real nervous and scared because of the weather. They each loaded a bunch more stuff in the trunk. It was getting really cramped. Judy explained to the girls in the car that she had to put me in a black garbage bag and squish me in the trunk. I can hear them laughing. They must think it is funny. Then I could hear the girls talking. They wonder what they will tell Rose about me being stuffed in the trunk of the car. Should they tell her what they did to me or not? They wonder how Rose will feel about the girls after learning what they did to me. Why not just tell her the truth? It is the best way. I can hear them giggling again.

I said, "Judy, Judy, I am still having trouble breathing. Can anyone hear me? Jan? Anybody?"

Nope. No one can hear me, but I can hear them talking about the pouring rain, snow and the slush on the road. Everyone sounds very nervous. I know it is a long drive because I was there last month. Finally, we stopped.

Judy opened the trunk and was moving some of the bags around.

"Can I get out now?" I asked.

"Sorry, Sassy, but you have to stay here," Judy said.

"No! NO! Why can't I go inside? Where are we?" I asked.

Judy told me that no dogs are allowed inside the building. She said that there was a big sign that said "NO DOGS ALLOWED." I don't remember that sign the last time I was here. Maybe it is a new sign, or maybe just an excuse not to take me with them. She said that the girls could get into a lot of trouble taking me in the building and did not want me sitting out in the pouring rain. I hate these plastic bags. It is hard to breathe and I am stuck here in the dark all by myself. It was a long wait until the girls returned. Judy opened the trunk and they put their bags back in the trunk and then I really got squished into a corner. All the girls all climbed back in the car, and we finally started to move again.

We stopped at a town called Fairview. Judy got out of car, opened the trunk and grabbed the big black bag that I was cramped in and lifted me out. Finally, I am out of that horrible black stinky bag! I was so cold that I think I turned blue in there. I was carried into a real nice restaurant. The girls found a big table right next to a beautiful fireplace. I got to sit on a little shelf right next to it. Ooh, this is nice and warm. My bum, tail, feet, nose and ears are finally warmed up. I'm purple again!

I met more new ladies, including a group of Red Hatters from a big city called Grande Prairie. They sure looked at me for a long time to try to figure out why these girls thought I was special and take me with them on outings. They would never do that with their mascot. I met a new lady, too; she is not a Red Hatter yet, but she is thinking about joining the group from her town. Maybe if I wink at her, smile a lot, and wiggle my ears and tail she just might want to join. Oh boy, here comes that camera again that flashes and gives me spots in front of my eyes. I am finally getting used to them now though.

Everyone has warmed up, finished eating and had a coffee or tea, so it is time to get back on the road and head home. Judy picked me up, carried me outside, opened the trunk and grabbed the two big plastic bags. Here I go, back into those bags and in the tiny corner of the trunk. I can hear the girls talking again and now they are really hesitant to tell Rose what they did to me. It was a slow trip back because of the slush on the road. Finally, we are back in Peace River. Judy drove around and dropped off all the girls at their homes, and then we finally got back to her place. It is still raining. She took me and the bags from the trunk and carried me inside her house. She took me out of the bags and set me back on the couch with my teddy friends. Finally, I can breathe again.

Hey teddies, have I ever got a story to tell you.

Rose came to Judy's to pick me up and take me back to her place. Judy told her a little of what happened with the bad weather, the roads and of course the trunk. Rose took me to the car, opened the door and buckled me in the back seat of her car.

"Hey, Rose, you are not going to believe the day that I had," I said.

Finally, I am back at Rose's place. She said that all the ladies who went for the trip decided that I should live with her, and her title should be Mascot Mum because she was responsible for finding, buying and rescuing me from boredom. I will be visiting Red Hat members, they will tell Rose what happened to me during the visit and she will keep a diary of all the events. What an adventure I had today! I wonder where I will go now.

CHAPTER 3

I have been waiting for something to happen again with the Red Hat ladies. Finally Rose told me that we are going out to a restaurant. She is dressed up real nice and is wearing a red hat of course. She even pinned a fancy hat on me. Judy is picking us up in her car, and Jan is with her. I got buckled into the back seat again. I am getting used to the seat belt now. We all went to a restaurant called TJ's. There were a bunch of ladies there, including a new lady who wants to join our group. Christine is here too, and she brought a little brown bag of goodies for everyone, including me.

"Thank you, Christine," I said.

There is a big white square thing on the wall with a picture that is moving. Rose explained that it is a movie screen and we are going to be watching a movie. There were some older ladies from England on the screen without clothes on. The movie was stopped until everyone had something to eat, and then the owner of TJ's came back and restarted the movie. It is called *Calendar Girls*. It is about some older ladies that pose nude for a calendar. So, "nude" means "with no clothes on." I sat in a chair and watched the whole movie. It was sure good. Someone took a picture of the group of ladies at the end of the movie. I am learning to accept the flashes from the camera now, and I try to smile like everyone else.

The ladies were talking about maybe looking into making our own Red Hat calendar with pictures of events and parties that we all attended. Nothing nude though. They did say they would make sure that I am in some pictures too.

Rose took me to Judy's place for a couple of days because there is a Christmas tree work bee happening again. She has to work and cannot help. She brought some things with her though to help decorate the tree. When we got to Judy's house, she unbuckled me and took me and the bag of goodies to the door and rang the bell. She gave me and the decorations to Judy and then said she had to leave. Judy and I went downstairs, and she sat me on that comfortable couch with the teddies again.

Sometime later, I heard footsteps heading my way. Judy peeked around the corner at me.

"What are we doing now Judy?" I asked.

"You'll see," she said.

She picked me up, took me outside and set me on a big lawn chair. The day was warm and sunny, so it was nice to breathe fresh air. Judy has two small pets that make a yipping noise. I have heard them yip before, but this is my first real contact with them. She explained that they are dogs and they love to bark. Hey, I am a dog too, but I sure look different compared to them.

"Hey, you two dogs, careful now, sniffing is allowed, but biting isn't. Remember, I am bigger than you are," I said.

Judy went back into the house and then came out with her camera and took pictures of me and her pet dogs.

"Judy, where are you putting me? What is this skinny little thing you are trying to set me on?" I asked.

She said that it is a fence. It is so high up in the air and so skinny I am not sure that I will fit. I may even overbalance, fall off and then the dogs might attack me. Judy mumbles something. She put me back on the chair and then went back into the house and brought out a little blanket. She put it on the rail and then wiggled me around so that I would not fall off. Boy, can I ever see a lot of different flowers and trees from this height. Sure is pretty. She even took pictures of me "fence sitting," as she called it.

We sat outside for quite a while enjoying the sunshine. She even got up, bent over and pulled some little green things out of the ground from between the flowers. She called them weeds. Judy took this great big long skinny green thing, turned a handle and then water came gushing out of it. She put the water on the flowers. She explained that she has to water the flowers when the soil gets dry so that the plants can grow and not die. When she was done, we went back in the house and I sat with the teddies.

I think that it is time to have fun again because Judy is dressed in purple and is wearing a little red hat. She put my hat on with a pin. It does not hurt anymore. Jan arrived and came into the house. She picked up me, and then Judy and I sat in the back seat and buckled in. Jan drove around town and then stopped and picked up Joyce. Now we are all heading to Christine's to decorate the tree for the Festival of Trees. What does it mean to decorate something? Sure hope it is a fun thing to do.

We drove over that big holey bridge, then onto that bumpy road and here comes that big hill. My stomach did a flip flop again. Thank goodness for seat belts. We finally got to Christine's.

There are a lot of ladies here, and they sure are doing a lot of talking about decorations. Jan set me on a chair so that I could see everything that was going on. The ladies set up the big green tree. So that is what our Christmas tree is going to look like! They put teddies on the tree and then added purple beads and little purple flowers. They tried little dresses and boas, but it did not give it any glamour.

I said, "Hey, girls, why not try some silver balls. I bet they would look good."

There was a ceremony called a "reduation" held today too. What a strange word, it sounds like a Red Hat word. Yep, it is. It is a special ceremony celebrating when a Red Hat lady turns fifty. Beth is now fifty years old, so she is now an official Red Hatter. After a speech, Christine presented her with a special

Red Hat. Everyone clapped their hands and then gave her a big welcome hug. I did too.

It is lunchtime and boy, I sure am hungry. Everything looks great. There is angel food cake, blueberries, strawberries and whipped cream. Drinks were coffee, tea and juice.

I am going to stay here with Christine for a while instead of going back to town with the girls. The girls decided that the hostess will decide at the next event who I will visit. Boy, this sounds like fun. I will get to go to a lot of different places and meet a lot of people. I wonder if any other Red Hat mascots do this. I have not heard any other stories like mine.

Rose keeps writing up my story and then adds it into an album. She added pictures and other things like flower stickers and feathers for decorations, making it look like a scrapbook album. Whenever I visit someone, that lady can read what has happened to me and the Sassy REDs.

Later that evening, Christine's husband picked up the album, sat down at the table and read my story. He started to laugh. He looked at me and said that he loved the story and thought the part about me being squished in the garbage bags in the trunk of the car was the best part.

"That was scary!" I replied.

He just smiled and then winked at me.

Christine is putting a nice little hat on me. That must mean we are going somewhere again.

"Hey, Christine, where are we going?" I asked.

"We are going for coffee with the girls at Travellers," she said.

She took me to the car, buckled me in the back seat and then got in the car. She started it and away we went back to town. Again my tummy did the flip flops going up and down that big hill. We drove through some green lights and finally got to the restaurant. We always get to sit at this special big round table. It is reserved just for us Red Hat ladies by John Vogt, the manager. He has been very supportive of us girls and makes sure that everything is just right. He has even stopped by a couple of times just to say hello.

There is a new girl here; she will be a Pink Hatter if she decides to join our group.

As usual, I was sitting on the table when the waitress came over, looked at me and came up with an idea. She brought over a special little chair. It is called a high chair and is used for little children when they come to this restaurant. She sat me in it, and it was perfect for me. I like this chair, and I would love to use it every time I go out with the girls. Everyone agreed that it was a great chair just for me.

All the ladies either had coffee or tea. The girls talked again about the tree decorating.

I looked up and in walked Judy and Ruth.

"Hey, are my eyes playing tricks on me? Why are Judy and Ruth wearing purple hats and red outfits instead of red hats and purple outfits?" I asked.

Judy said, "When it is your birthday month, you wear opposite colours."

What a great idea! You get to wear reverse colours when it is your birthday. When is my birthday? I think it is in April. I have lots of red hats. I would love to have a purple hat for my birthday month. I will talk to Rose about it.

We all had a good visit, and now it is time to leave. I am going to visit with Joyce for a while now. I have not been to her place yet. I wonder if she has any dogs, cats or other types of pets. Joyce is driving Rose home tonight. She took me out to her van and buckled me in. After we dropped Rose off at her home, we went back to her place. Joyce picked me up and carried me into her home. I looked around a bit. Hey, no pets!

I was sitting on a couch when I heard something—it sounded like a bunch of feet running towards me. Oh, look, here come a bunch of little people. There are one, two, three, four, five little girls. Joyce said that they are her granddaughters. They are sure excited to see me and are sure looking me over. They squish my nose, tickle my feet and ears and point and giggle at my eyes.

They went away, and when they came back they were carrying a big bright red helmet and a pair of huge plastic goggles. The one girl put the helmet on my head, and another girl put the goggles over my eyes. They said that I was going to be a flag person in training.

"What kind of training?" I asked.

They said that I will learn how to direct cars. *Direct cars? Me?*

The little girls pretended that they were driving cars, and when they came close to me they stopped, waited and then drove off again. What a fun game! Joyce even took pictures.

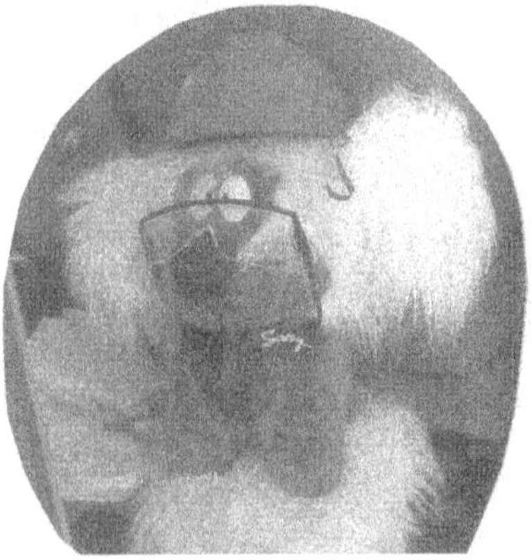

I am a Flag Person in Training.

The next day, Joyce picked me up and carried me to a little room.

"Joyce, hey, Joyce, where are you taking me?" I asked.

She set me on a top shelf in a small room that has a big white thing with a door that she puts clothes into. She added some blue stuff into a little slot. Joyce said that it is soap to clean the clothes. She called it a washing machine. After a while, the clothes come out wet. She then puts the wet clothes into another big, white machine, adds a little paper thing, and they come out dry. She said that one is a dryer. They both made a humming noise. There is a round window on the front of the dryer, and I can see the clothes tumbling a lot. It is a good thing that I am outside and not inside of that machine.

Joyce's husband is a quiet guy.

"Hello, there. Hi. Hey," I said. Nope, he did not even notice me.

Joyce is all dressed up and wearing a little red hat.

"Hey, where are you going?" I asked her.

She looked at me, waved and sort of slinked away really fast.

"Can I go too? Can I? Can you hear me? Joyce. Joyce!" I shouted.

Nope. I heard her footsteps across the floor and then heard the door shut. I think that she snuck out the door figuring that I would not see or hear her leave. I wonder where she is going. I think it is coffee night again. I will just wait for her to come back.

She is back now. She saw me waiting for her on the couch. Joyce walked over to me and told me that some of the ladies went out for tea and coffee. She did not take me because it was cold outside and I would have needed a big heavy coat to keep warm. She did not want me to get a chill, start to cough and sneeze and end up getting pneumonia.

Joyce said that she is going to take me to an "orange night party." She gave me a cute orange pumpkin hat to wear that she bought earlier. Judy is here to pick us up for the party. Joyce picked me up and carried me to the car. She opened the back door, set me on the back seat, shut the door and then got in the front seat with Judy. She forgot to put on my seat belt!

I asked, "What about my seat belt?"

They were talking and did not hear me. I sure hope that I do not fall over. Hey, we are picking up Rose too. It was dark in the car, so Rose also did not notice that I was not in the seat belt. We finally arrived at the party house. We all got out of the car, walked to the house and knocked on the door. There are lots of ladies here. Let me count and see how many are here. I can count to twenty now. One, two, three, four, five, what number comes after five? I heard someone say that there are thirteen ladies here. Wow! What a turnout! It is the best turnout ever. I must be the next number. Let's see, four comes after three, so fourteen must come after thirteen. There are fourteen of us here having fun.

Ruth gave me an orange amulet necklace, and Christine gave me ear muffs and some orange socks. The socks are too small for me because I have big feet.

Jan is here too. She has purple hair tonight. She called it a wig. Hey, it is close to my colour. She sure looks different.

Ruth invented a little game for the ladies. She had a bunch of black and white pictures of couples on their wedding day and also on their fiftieth and sixtieth wedding anniversary. We had to match them up. In the first round, the ladies only got two couples right. People change appearances more than dogs do I guess. It looked like a simple game to me. I tried to help, but the ladies were so excited that they couldn't hear me.

This is a special night because there is a lunar eclipse. All the ladies are excited. What's an eclipse? Rose picked me up and took me outside so that I could see what all the excitement was about. I had my new earmuffs on so my ears would not get cold. There was snow on the ground. It was a good thing that Rose was carrying me because I would have gotten my feet wet. We all found a perfect spot to see the moon. There it was, way up in the dark sky, and it looked reddish and fuzzy. It looked like something black was crossing in front of the moon so that it was slowly vanishing, but still it was there. So, *that's* an eclipse! This does not happen very often, and sometimes people cannot enjoy it because there are a lot of clouds in the sky. This was a perfect night for this event. We started to get cold, so we all walked back into the house.

The table is decorated with orange and black candles. There are orange carrot sticks and peppers to snack on. Everyone had angel food cake, orange Jell-O and a drink.

Ruth said that she went to Tim Horton's coffee shop a few times and got a special coin for all the girls. It is a special quarter that has a red poppy in the centre of it. The quarter is a commemorative coin in honour of our war dead. The Royal Canadian Mint launched the world's first coloured coin on October 21, 2004. Wow, this is history in the making! I think that it is great. Christine bought all the girls a Halloween pencil, and Helen brought kazoos. The kazoo is the official musical instrument of the Red Hat Society. It was Ruth's birthday yesterday, so all the girls played "Happy Birthday" on their kazoos for her.

Every lady brought a wrapped gift, and they were all put on the floor. Everyone drew a number and then chose a gift. The budget was supposed to be ten dollars, but I am sure that some ladies do not know how much that is because a lot of the gifts looked like they were a lot more than that. A few ladies took gifts away from each other. It is a game called the "Chinese Gift Exchange." Wow, some of the gifts were sure beautiful. There was everything from a cake, candles, tea towels, roosters and even an orange teddy bear.

A lot of pictures were taken again, including a group photo. No more dots in front of my eyes from the flashes.

I am going to stay with Ruth and visit with her for a while. It was sure a fun party.

Ruth has a small pet dog whose name is Winks. He is very excited and is making me *real* nervous. He reminds me of Rose's cat, Casper. Ruth tried to take a picture of me with her dog, but he would not cooperate. Oh good, she is putting me in a safe place so that Winks cannot attack me.

Ruth talked to me about Halloween. She said that children get dressed up in costumes, go to houses and get candies. Sounds like a fun time.

"Can I get dressed up too?" I asked. "I have ear muffs, socks, a pumpkin hat and a necklace that I can wear."

"Sure," said Ruth.

She put on my pumpkin hat and necklace and sat me on a chair by her window so I could see the children come to the door. Boy, there sure are a lot of them. The kids started to come just before it got dark and then stopped after a couple of hours. I even had my picture taken with some of them. They thought I was cute. They had on such nice costumes that I would have gone with them, but I decided against it. I did not want to get lost and not be able to find my way back. Halloween is sure a fun night.

Welcome to Orange Night.

I like visiting with Ruth. She gave me a red flower to wear. She said it is a poppy. People wear poppies to remember the people who fought in the war for our freedom. That day is

November 11 and it is called Remembrance Day. It sounds very special. I am so proud to wear this poppy.

So Proud to Wear a Poppy

Ruth is busy packing my hats, goodies and album into a box and a bag.

"Where are we going?" I asked her.

She said, "It is a surprise. You will just have to be patient and wait."

Ruth said something to me the other day about the Festival of Trees. Maybe we are going there. The girls have been working hard to make that tree beautiful. I know that you have to purchase tickets in advance to attend this gala function. That cost thing could be a problem for me again, so I might not be able to attend.

Ruth packed all my things into the car and then came back and got me. The girls sure have been buying me a lot of neat things to wear. Soon I will need something to keep all my stuff in instead of bags and boxes. She put me on the front seat with her and buckled me in. Finally, she told me that it is the opening night of the Festival of Trees, and that is where we are going. I sure am excited. This is my first time going to this grand event. Ruth drove to the Travellers building, got out of the car, opened my door, unbuckled me and took me inside the big building.

Wow! Look at this place. It is the ballroom of the Travellers hotel. The room is all aglitter for Christmas with lights and other decorations. There are a lot of people in here working on their trees. There are lots of other things here too, like quilts and gingerbread houses. Lots of the Sassy REDs are here too. They are making our tree beautiful. There are one, two, three—uh, there are just too many ladies here to count them all. I heard someone say that there are eleven ladies here.

Merry Christmas

Hello, teddies. I remember these fuzzy animal friends; they sure look great under and on the tree. The girls decided that I can stay under the tree with my friends. They got permission from the organizers of the event and put me on a little pedestal with a sign that said that I am the Sassy RED's mascot and not to be included in the auction. Whew, that is good because I do not want to be sold. I will stay here for a couple of days and protect the tree for the ladies. The Sassy REDs even brought a big red boa wreath with a white ribbon on it for a raffle.

Rose came back that evening and brought me a cute little bracelet with my name on it. It just fits on my right leg. She said that it is an early Christmas present.

It sure is quiet here with everyone gone and the place all locked up. I am going to take a little nap. Teddy bears, Christmas tree, auction, talking, Christmas lights and food and drink. I opened my eyes. The teddies said that I was wiggling and laughing. It must be another dream.

Here come the judges, and they are carrying ribbons to hand out. Are they going to stop at our tree? Nope, that means we did not win a prize, but I wonder if our tree will go up for auction or just for highest bid.

It is finally gala night for Festival of Trees. I am so excited to be here. Here come all the ladies. There are nine of them, and they are all dressed up with special hats, boas, shawls and even gloves. What a gorgeous sight! It is like a sea of purple and red. They sure stand out from everyone else who is wearing just regular clothes. Wow, there are sure a lot of people here. The place is packed, and there is not enough room for everyone to sit down. It is a good thing that the ladies came early and got to sit at a big round table.

"Hey, girls, where are you going?" I asked.

They did not hear me and got up and moved over to get their picture taken sitting by a thing that has a whole bunch of white and black things on it. I heard someone called it a piano. Now they are going to another section for another group picture.

"What about me?" I asked again.

I sit under the tree. I think that they got so excited that they forgot about me. Oh well, I enjoy the attention from all the people who look at our tree and me as well. I can hear people talking and giggling about my eyes. I just sat there and smiled at them.

The ladies finally came back to their table. A man came over and talked to them. He was from the radio station KIX and wanted to know about our group of fun-loving, fifty-and-older ladies who like to dress up and have fun. Judy explained to him about the tree, the Sassy REDs group and their mascot. Me.

Our tree went up for auction next. The bid kept going higher and higher. The girls were sure excited. They spent about $350 on the tree. Wow, it sold for $750 to a lady from the dentist's office. That sure is a lot of money for a decorated Christmas tree! The girls are so happy. I am going to stay here for a couple of days until the festival is over.

I loved being under the tree; I sure got to meet a lot of people. Rose came and picked me up to take me to a special coffee meeting in a different part of the building. There are lots of ladies here. Someone said that there are twelve. Yep, looks like that many. There are three new ladies here too. I was introduced to them, but there are too many names to remember. They sure asked a lot of questions about me.

The Festival of Trees is now over for the year, so Rose takes me back to her place because she is having her annual Christmas party soon.

She took me to the car, put me on the front seat, buckled me in and then got in the car and drove home. She put me on the floor with all her snowmen and took a bunch of pictures. She is still working on that album for me, too, with all my adventures and, of course, pictures.

Her cat, Casper, is eyeing me again.

"Scat, cat! I'm bigger than you are," I said.

Rose did not want him around in case he started eating things, so she chased him into another room. I wish I could do that to him sometimes, too.

She has a huge five-foot-tall red Christmas stocking for her party. She thought that it would be a fun idea if she put me in the stocking. She picked me up and then measured me. I looked too big to fit, so she started to bend me out of shape.

"Ouch! Ouch!" I said. "It is not going to work. My feet are too big for the little hole in the top of the stocking," I explained.

"I will make you fit," she said.

She squishes and twists me, still trying to make me fit. No matter what she did, it did not work, so she finally quit and had to think of another idea. I am sure she will think of something.

Now *That's* a Stocking!

It sure is quiet here today with Burt and Rose both gone to work. Oh my, here comes Casper, and it looks like there could be some problems. He walked across the floor, got real close to me and then he lifted his paw.

"Help! Help! HELP! Can someone hear me? Casper, that grey and white beastly cat with huge teeth, is going to attack me!" I yelled.

He batted me really hard with his paw several times and finally knocked me off my favourite chair, and I fell down onto the floor with a thump. I landed on my side. Casper was not expecting that, so he jumped about a foot in the air from being startled. Boy, did I ever scare him! He slowly walked back over to me and then stuck his teeth into my ear and started to drag me across the floor. I am sure he had a smirk on his face when he did this. He did it slowly because I am a lot bigger than he is.

"Help. Get lost, cat! Vamoose! Leave me alone!" I hollered.

Nope, he was not quite done with me yet. He sunk his teeth into my right foot. He sure has big teeth. He shook me back and forth so that now I was lying on my back. He stopped, stared at me and then whacked me on my head again. Then he started to chew my other leg. The silver in my fur is sure attracting him. He spit out some of my silver hair onto the floor a couple of times. I hope he gets really sick from all that silver stuff. He took his paw and whacked my head again a couple more times. Thank heavens he does not have claws in his front paws. Then he used those sharp teeth again, only this time they sunk into my puffy nose. He shook me again.

Casper the Attack Cat

"Stop! Stop! Casper, you have done enough to me," I screamed.

He stopped shaking me and stared at me again. He got real close to my face. His eyes are sure big and green. We had a staring contest. I think I won. He turned his head, breaking the staring contest and then whacked me on my puffy nose one last time.

Finally, he decided that he had enough fun with me, and he went walking into the kitchen and left me lying on my back in the middle of the floor. I wonder what Rose will think happened to me when she gets home.

I hear someone coming. It's Rose. She is home early.

"Thank goodness you are home," I said.

"Sassy, what happened to you?" she asked.

She was sure surprised when she saw me lying on my back in the middle of the room. She walked over, picked me up, carefully checked me over and could not find any big holes or major damage. She even picked up the bits of silver and white fuzz that Casper left behind on the floor. Yep. She figured out that Casper did a number on me. She then put me up on a high place so Casper could not reach me. Thank goodness this frightening experience will not happen again.

A few days later, Rose picked me up, put a nice little hat on me and said that we were going out.

"Where are we going? Rose, where are you taking me?" I asked.

"I want you to meet some of my friends from work," she said.

While at work, she told her coworkers about me and they were interested in meeting me. We left the building, she opened the car door and sat me in the front seat and buckled me in. She got in, started the car and made a couple of stops in town. Then she drove up that big hill with the holey bridge and water under it and we finally got to where she works. Boy, is it ever a huge store. There is a sign on the door that says "No Dogs Allowed."

"Oh, no! Not again about the dog rule," I mumbled.

I said to her, "Why not just hide me in a plastic bag so you will not get into trouble."

She liked that idea, so she opened the trunk and found a plastic bag. She stuck me in the little bag, shut the trunk and then we walked into the store. When she got to the bakery, she took me out of the plastic bag, set me on the counter and introduced me to Tiffany and Stacey. They do packaging and bread slicing at the bakery. Their eyes lit up, and they giggled, both with big smiles on their faces. They loved me! Tiffany hugged me and asked me if I wanted a cookie. The bakery department hands out free cookies to children who come shopping with their parents. Tiffany handed me the plate of cookies, and I took a red Christmas cookie. Rose explained that the "No Dogs Allowed" sign on the door was the reason for the plastic bag. Both of the girls insisted that I did not have to go back in the bag because I was too cute and no one would complain or report me to the management.

After the visit, Rose picked me up and we went looking for the lady that does the cake decorating because she wanted to meet me too. We looked all over the store and even stopped in at the cafeteria, but could not find her. I did meet a lady that used to work in the bakery with Rose but had moved to a different section of the store. What a big store, and there were sure a lot of people shopping and working here. The store is open all the time and only closes for Christmas day.

Rose's main boss even walked by us and said, "Cute thing." I just smiled at him.

Rose found a little black basket with a handle on it. It is used to carry things that you want to buy. She put me in it and then found a couple of items that she wanted to purchase. We stood in a lineup of people who were buying things too. They looked at me and giggled. Rose explained that I am the mascot for the Sassy REDs and she brought me here for an adventure. There is a round turning table to get items close to the person at the till.

It moves when the person at the till hits a little button. I watched it move the food items.

I asked, "Can I have fun and go on a little ride?"

Rose agreed, and so did the lady at the till. I took a little ride.

"That was fun. Can I do it again?" I asked.

I got three little rides because the lady at the till smiled, giggled and agreed to it too. The lady put the items in a bag, and Rose paid for them. We left the store, got in the car, buckled up and went home.

Rose is sure busy doing things for her party. She put a red hat with an arrow at the top of the stairs so that the ladies know which way to go to find her apartment. She even put a beautiful red hat on her door!

I can hear some knocking on the door. Here come the ladies all dressed up and bringing hats and wrapped items. There was a hat contest again, and even my hat was included. Judy's hat won the contest. She got a little purple reindeer with a red hat for a prize. Everyone had to bring a purple gift worth exactly $3.59 with a receipt as proof and then put them into that big red stocking that Rose tried to stuff me into. Rose came up with this $3.59 idea because of the confusion at the Halloween party when everyone had to bring a gift worth ten dollars and a lot of gifts were worth more than that. There were a lot of gifts, and they filled the huge stocking. Christine and Jan were the only two ladies who did not spend the exact amount. The girls thought the amount was fun and it took a while to find items that added up to $3.59. They want to do this game again in July when she has her Christmas in July party.

Rose had her tree decorated with red shoes that she made from felt material. The shoes were all decorated with little bows, flowers and some shiny stuff. The ladies each got to pick one. She also gave each lady a shiny red poinsettia flower corsage too.

Christine won the door prize, which was a candy cane house with "Joy" on the bottom. She was so surprised and happy.

Judy hummed on her kazoo and the ladies sang two Red Hatter Christmas songs. Rose planned two games, one of which was a trivia game. The first letters spelled out the answer, which was "Merry Christmas." Wendy won and received a crystal mug. The second game was easy; the ladies had to guess how many snowmen Rose had. Sally won, and Rose has 47 snowmen! Wow.

Judy brought some gifts for a "left and right" game. She told the story of the Right family, and the girls stood in a circle to hand gifts from the left or right according to the story. Jan brought everyone a fuzzy purple pen. I sat in the middle of the floor and all the gifts were put around me. Of course pictures were taken. This was sure a fun day. Jan brought me a beautiful pin with my name on it. Oh Jan, I am getting tears in my eyes. It is so shiny and pretty. Rose pinned it on my collar.

Christine brought a funny looking three-legged stand. She put her camera on it to take a group picture. She tried and tried but could not figure out how the timer worked, so Rose talked to a lady in the apartment building who came and took pictures of all of us. It sure was a busy evening. It was cold outside at thirty degrees below zero. At Rose's Christmas in July, it was thirty above. What a difference! It is about nine in the evening so all the girls are leaving now. I wonder who I will visit with next.

"Hey! Ladies! Ladies! Am I staying here with Rose or am I going with one of you?" I asked. No answer.

The ladies are all excited and are not even thinking about me. I guess I will stay with Rose and then she can take me to the Elvis night, which is happening soon.

Hmm, Rose has on a red hat and purple top. I wonder where she is going. It must be coffee night again. I heard that it is real cold out again so Rose said that it would be better for me to stay home where it is nice and warm. This is the last meeting of the year. What a year it has been.

I wonder what next year will be like.

CHAPTER 4

Rose put a little hat on me and then took me to the usual coffee meeting at Travellers. Everyone is so excited and wishing everyone a Happy New Year. Rose had explained to me earlier about the change from one year to another and everyone celebrating. I got to sit in that special little high chair again. The ladies were talking about what they did for Christmas with their families.

I am going to Joyce's place again. She took me to her car, buckled me in and we drove slowly to her place. There was a lot of snow on the roads. I wonder if her granddaughters will be there again. We got to her place, and when we walked into the house I did not see the little girls, but I did see her husband.

"Hi. Hello. Hi," I said.

Again he did not notice me. Joyce is getting ready for her "Elvis night." Who is this famous person? She has a bunch of items and pictures of a good-looking, black-haired young man. He must be Elvis, the "King of Rock and Roll." What is rock? What is roll? I guess I will find out later.

All the ladies arrive, and some of them are dressed up in costumes. Again Christine brought her camera and three-legged stand and takes a bunch of pictures. She is now our official picture taker, and she has figured out how to set the timer so she can be in the pictures too.

Celebrating Elvis

Everyone was supposed to bring an "Elvis item" for show and tell. Most of the ladies did. Rose brought a cutting board that said "Elvis Parsley" on it. Everyone thought it was unique. There were newspaper articles and records on display for the ladies to look at. Jan bought them when she was in the United States. The television was on and it was playing some videos of Elvis's concerts. Oh, he sure was a handsome young man with a very special voice and wiggle! We learned that his favourite food was a peanut butter sandwich.

Everyone was given a red cardboard hat with a feather connected to it as a keepsake. Lunch was a veggie platter, fruits, cheese, crackers and even a mini angel food cake with strawberries, and there was coffee, tea and mulled wine to drink. We even watched a movie starring Elvis. He sure sings a lot in his movies. What a fun evening. I sure learned a lot about Elvis and rock and roll.

I am still staying with Joyce for a while. I can hear little footsteps again. Yep, here come three of her granddaughters to play with me. They are playing with my ears and making them go up and down. One girl tickles my feet and another twitches my tail at the same time. Do I wiggle or giggle? This is fun. It has been a long time since I played with these little girls.

Joyce is all dressed up in purple and wearing a special red hat. She brought over one of my nice hats for me to wear.

"Where are we going?" I asked her.

She said, "We are all going out for a meal."

"Am I going to need money?" I asked.

Joyce said that it would be her treat if I consumed anything and that the cafe is a real nice place to eat. We went out to her car she put me on the front seat, got in the driver's seat and took off for the restaurant. She forgot the seatbelt again. Joyce steered around a sharp corner, and I fell over and my puffy nose hit the door handle.

"Ouch," I said.

Joyce reached over and set me straight again. She apologized, saying that she forgot about the seat belt. We are meeting at the Sunflower Café and there are fourteen ladies there. There is a lot of artwork on display. The meal was sure good. I got to sit in a big upholstered chair that is nice and soft and comfy. We all talked and then left at about nine in the evening.

It is coffee night again at Travellers. Joyce picked me up, stuck a pin through my little hat, and took me with her, even though it is cold outside. Maybe I should look into buying a fur coat to wear for the cold weather. Another new lady is here. This group is sure growing so big and so fast that I am having some trouble remembering all the different names. Some names are even the same. Maybe everyone should wear name tags. I do.

After drinking coffee and saying goodbye to everyone, Joyce put me in the front seat of her car and remembered to buckled me in and then drove to Jan's place. She took me to the house, rang the doorbell and gave me to Jan who is planning a Hawaiian night. I am here a bit early so that I can help her.

Jan's husband walked in the room and she introduced me to him.

"Sassy, meet my husband Heinz," she said.

I smiled at him. He smiled, said hi to me and then giggled. It must be my eyes. He picked me up and carried me into the theatre room where we sat together and watched a movie on TV. It was quite late in the evening, so he fell asleep on the couch and then I did too. Tomorrow is the big day, Hawaiian style!

Heinz helps by preparing the food and Jan decorates the house. I am sitting and watching them and giving them some advice at times. There are some real funny looking trees. One is even purple and the other is green. Jan called them palm trees. Finally, everything is ready, so Jan and I sat down to wait for the ladies to show up. Everyone was asked to arrive dressed in special outfits that are real colourful and bright.

I got Lei-ed!

Christine went to Hawaii for a holiday and brought back a bunch of shelled and flowered leis. She came early so that she could present them to the girls as they walked in the door, just like they do in Hawaii. Jan held me, and Christine put both leis on me. I was so proud. All the girls had to be barefoot because a lady had a special gift of a Hawaiian snowshoe for everyone. A picture was taken of all the feet. Jan found everyone's name in the Hawaiian language and put it on a name tag. She could not find "Sassy" though, so I did not get one.

The house is so nicely decorated. There are even special mats on the floor so that we feel as if we are walking on sand. Some ladies told stories about Hawaii, and Judy told one about how she got her hat. All the ladies stood up and we played a "pass the coconut game," and the winner was Michelle, who won a straw hat. The next game that was played required the ladies to write a telegram using only certain words. That winner won a straw hat too.

Lunch was mini spare ribs, fruits, veggies, crackers and even Hawaiian punch to drink.

Goodbye, everyone. That sure was a fun party.

"Hey, Jan," I said. "It is midnight, and it is time both of us got some sleep."

She agreed, took me upstairs and put me on a real comfy couch. I shut my eyes, and then there I was, walking on the beach, drinking punch and attending a luau. My eyes opened—I was having a beautiful Hawaiian dream.

The next morning, Jan took me to a special little place; she called it her dressing room. It is where she sits and puts makeup on before she goes to work. She has lots of bling and things that I will look after while she is gone. She told me that someday real soon she will even take me to work with her.

Jan is getting dressed in purple and looking at all her hats and trying to pick the right one for tonight.

"Where are we going now, Jan?" I asked.

She said, "It is coffee night again at Travellers."

Jan picked me up, walked out to the car, buckled me in and then she got in and drove to Travellers. The waitresses are so nice to us that the ladies gave them each a little bag of goodies. My little chair was already in place, waiting for me to sit in it. It is a lot of fun sitting and listening to the girls tell stories about what is happening in their lives.

"Who will I visit with now? I asked.

Darla picked me up and said, "It's my turn."

Darla works at the post office. That is where you pick up the mail and send out letters.

We got to her place, got out of the car and walked into her house. I heard a whole bunch of barking. It sounded like there were six dogs. I looked, and there were only two of them. Darla took me downstairs so we could watch television.

Boy, it is sure warm in here. There is a big wood-burning heater in the corner. That is why it is so warm. We sat and watched a sport that I had never seen before. Darla called it curling. Interesting game. After the game was over, Darla picked me up and showed me the two dog beds that she had for her pets. She put me in them. I fit! The dogs looked at me kind of funny so I told Darla that I would rather sit on the big chair.

One day, close to Saint Patrick's Day, Darla walked in the room and smiled at me.

"This is just special for you," she said. She showed me a special green hat that she bought for me to wear at the next coffee.

"I love it," I said. "Please put it on so that I can see what it is like."

She did, and then we walked into the bathroom and I looked in the mirror. I loved the hat!

Well, it is tea time again. Darla put on my green hat and away we went to Travellers. There are thirteen ladies here. Sally gave me some shiny green beads to wear. Joyce brought a little lamb that sang "When Irish Eyes Are Smiling." It was a great time. Darla said goodbye, and then Wanda said that it was her turn to take me.

We left Travellers and got into her vehicle, buckled up and drove to her house. We got out of the car and a big dog came up and started to sniff at me. I smiled at him and wiggled my tail and he wagged his. Good start to this friendship. We became instant friends.

Wanda's granddaughter came for a visit. She got all excited when she saw me. She grabbed my suitcase, opened it up and took my goodies out. She put the hats on my head and the boas around my neck. We were having a great time playing. She really loved the green beads. She tangled them around me in places that I did not know I had.

I stayed in the spare room. It had lots of toys in it so I had lots of company and time to chat with the rest of the new friends. I explained that I travelled a lot and told them some of the stories of things that happened to me.

Well, tea time again. Wanda got dressed up, put a hat on me and out the door we went. There are eleven ladies here tonight. We discuss plans for the book signing, international supper, and the Big Bike Ride. There are a lot of events going on in the next couple of months.

I will be going to Connie's this time. I have not been there before. She picked me up and carried me to her vehicle. It was a big black truck. It sure is high, and there is a special little step to get into it. I got buckled in and she went around, got in, started the vehicle, put the seat belt on and away we drove.

We finally got to her place. It is a little white house with green trim. We walked in the house and she set me on a little stool, and said, "Good night. I will see you in the morning." And then she went to bed.

The next day she puttered for a while in the house and then she put my baseball cap on me and carried me outside to the truck.

"We are going to have some fun," she said to me.

I wonder what she is going to do now. She and I got in the truck and away we went. We stopped at this big park that had lots of things to play on. She parked the truck, and we got out of it. She locked it and then we walked into the park. There was a big slide, and she asked if I wanted to go down it. I had never done this before, so sure, let's do it. This should be fun. She set me on the top of the slide and down I went, flew off the end, landed on my bum and then leaned forward and ended up on my puffy nose. Connie giggled, wiped the dust off my nose and asked me if I wanted to do it again. Sure, one more time.

Down I went again, got to the bottom, tumbled through the air twice and as usual landed on my nose. She picked me up and looked at the swings. We walked over, and she put me in the little seat and pushed me. Up and down I went several times. She was careful how hard she pushed me.

She did not want me flying off the seat and crashing on the grass. This is sure fun. There were a bunch of children at the park too. They giggled and came running over when they saw me. Connie explained to them that I was a mascot. Connie took me out of the swing, and I looked over and saw a sandbox and thought I could have fun playing there.

"Can I play in the sandbox?" I asked.

Connie did not like the idea because I would get all dirty, so we had to find something else.

"Let's try the merry-go-round," said Connie.

We walked to the merry-go-round and she set me on it. She pushed the handle, and round and round I went. I started to get dizzy. My hat fell off and I almost fell over so she took me off it. We sat on a bench for a while and watched all the kids playing and having fun. She decided it was time to go home because it was real cloudy and it looked like it was going to rain.

We got back in the truck and she drove back to her place.

A few days later, she picked me up and took me to her kitchen and sat me on a chair. She said that she was going to make some cookies and thought I might like to watch how to do it.

"That sounds like fun," I said.

She brought out a bunch of ingredients, such as butter, flour, sugar, eggs and chocolate chips. Then came the measuring and stirring. Finally, she took a scoop and scooped the dough onto a big flat metal sheet. She put them in the hot oven, set the timer and then waited for them to bake. A buzzer went off and she took them out, scraped them off the tray onto a cooling rack and let them cool. We went to the other room together and sat down and munched on freshly baked chocolate chip cookies.

What a fun day. I wonder what will happen tomorrow.

CHAPTER 5

It is now April, my birthday month. I get to wear a purple hat and red outfit.

"Hey, Rose, it is my birthday month and I do not have a purple hat yet," I said.

"Okay, let's fix that little problem," she answered.

She picked me up, walked out the door and went to the car. She opened the door, buckled me in the front seat of the car and then we headed to a special store. This store, she said, is run by the Salvation Army. She picked me up, and we walked into the store and looked around for a hat. There were some people in the store, and they were looking at us kind of funny. Rose set me on a little counter and put a bunch of different hats on me. She figured that she could paint one if she had to. She had done that before. Rose finally found a floppy dark purple one, but it was way too big for my head. It flopped down over my eyes so I could not see anything. She figured that she could gather it, add some flowers and it would be great.

Rose took me and the hat to the lady at the till. She looked at us kind of funny, which is normal when I go into a store with one of the ladies. Rose explained that I was the Sassy REDs mascot and that it was my birthday month. She said that we were looking for a purple hat for me to wear. The lady at the till giggled, said that she'd heard about our group of ladies and then said that there was no charge because the hat was for me. I smiled at her and thanked her for the hat.

We left the store and went back to the car. After both of us were buckled in, Rose and I headed back home. When we got there, she sat me on a little chair. She went into her arts and crafts room and brought out a funny looking thing and a variety of flowers. She said it was a glue gun. She plugged the glue gun into an electric plug so that it would heat up the glue. While it was heating, she fussed with the hat and kept picking flowers and trying them on the hat. I am sure that she has done this kind of thing many times before. She sure spent a lot of time on the hat and then kept measuring it on my head so that it would look good and still fit me. She did a bunch of gluing to make it smaller and then finally decided what flowers would be on the hat. She glued on a variety of flowers.

When she was finally done, she put the hat on my head and picked me up. We walked into the bathroom and she held me up in front of the mirror. I looked at myself and, wow, did that hat ever look fantastic. Now I was ready for my birthday month.

Rose is all dressed up for the supper. She put on my purple hat and did not even have to put a pin in my head. I even had a little red boa around my neck. We went out to the car, got in and she drove to Travellers. We arrived and walked into the special room that the girls booked for the event. She found a place for me to sit so I could see everything that was going on. There are lots of ladies here for this special event. They all saw my new hat and loved it. I just smiled at them.

A young man named Vern is our server for tonight. He started the evening by pouring the ladies a glass of red or white wine. The appetizer is a sliced cucumber made into a bowl with shrimp, crab meat and greenery. There was rolled bacon, scallops and shrimp surrounding the bowl. Then the soup arrived. It sure looked good. The main course was steak, dauphinoise potatoes, baby carrots, broccoli and cauliflower. There was a lot of food. Most of the ladies could not eat it all. Then it was time for dessert. Wow! Look at that! It sure looks yummy. It is called strawberries Romanoff with lady fingers. The two chefs, Tanya and Thomas, served the meal.

While the girls were busy eating, talking and drinking, I was sitting on the end of a very long table. I looked over and saw a tall glass with some clear liquid in it. I was sure thirsty. Maybe it is water. I tiptoed over to have a look. It sure looks like water. I leaned forward a little bit to see if there was a smell to the liquid. I leaned forward a bit more, and when I sniffed, my puffy nose touched the glass, and it accidently tipped over.

"Oh no, what did I do?" I asked.

I looked at the girls. No one heard me talk or heard the glass fall over onto the table. All the ladies were still talking, eating and having fun. I saw the liquid moving on the table, and so I bent over and started to lick up the liquid real fast so the girls would not notice. What a strange taste! There was a burning sensation as I swallowed the liquid. What was that liquid? I leaned back and touched the edge of the chair. It is a good thing it was there because I would have fallen backwards off the table without it. A couple of minutes later, I got a funny feeling. *What is happening to me? I am feeling kind of tipsy*, I thought to myself. *Actually, I am feeling a lot tipsy.* I shook my head and my hat fell on the floor. I swayed back and forth, and my little red boa ended up on the floor too.

"Girsh, girlz, laddies," I stammered.

I cannot talk properly. I am slurring my words. Oh my, what have I done! The spilled liquid that I thought was water must have been something else. I know that some of the girls were drinking wine. It must be wine. It definitely was not water.

A couple of the ladies noticed me then and wondered what was happening to me.

"Sassy, are you okay?" One of the ladies asked.

"I, uh I dwinked shum fuzzy wather," I slurred.

My eyes are not focusing. My head feels weird. My feet are rubbery and my tail is wiggling.

Then the weirdest thing happened. My eyes crossed, my head bent forward and then, *boing*, I actually flipped over with my head on the table and my feet in the air. I was totally upside down. Now most of the girls are looking at me, pointing and giggling.

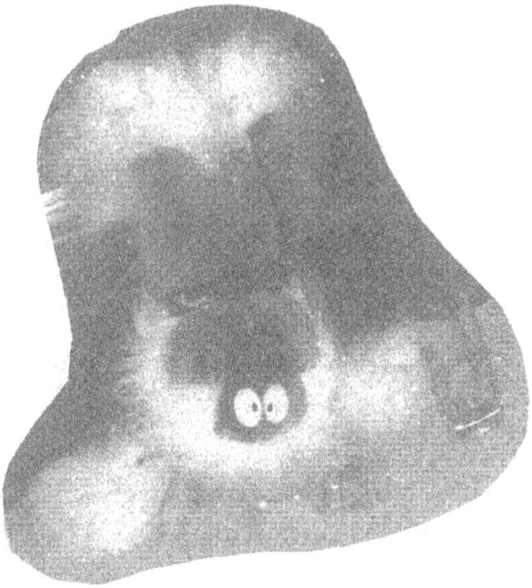

Tipsy Sassy

A lot of the girls brought out their cameras and took pictures of me with my head on the table and feet in the air. It was embarrassing, but the girls said that at some time or other everyone does something like this. It made me feel a little better, but I was still embarrassed. Someone finally came to my rescue and flipped me back to the right position. I am sitting back on the table now so the girls can watch me so that I do not get into any more trouble. I wobbled for a while and everything was swaying a little then slowly everything went back to normal. Boy, that was weird. John Vogt, the manager, even came and talked to us later in the evening. He wanted to make sure that everything was okay with our celebration.

At the end of the evening, the ladies and I all posed while a special photographer took our photo, and we all had our picture and write-up in the local newspaper. I was even in the picture, and my name was in the write-up. I got "inked!"

After the party, I went home with Lois.

It was a super party. At Lois's house later in the evening, I curled up on a comfy chair and went to sleep. Wine, balloons, wine, laughter, more wine, music, more wine, pictures and of course more wine. My eyes opened. I just had another dream.

The lady that owns the City Music bookstore in the mall invited the Red Hat ladies to set up a display in front of the store. The girls explained about me being their mascot and she loved the idea of me sitting in the window and watching people come into the store. There are even some books in the store about Red Hatters that are available for people to purchase.

Lois and I got in the car and drove to the Riverdrive Mall. We went to the store together and talked to the manager about me sitting in the window. She is a real nice lady. She went to the window and moved some books around so there would be room for me to sit and then put me on the window ledge. She brought a sign explaining that I was a mascot for the Sassy REDs. I watched a lot of people walk by. Some even stopped, pointed at me and waved. I just smiled back at them. I did this for a couple of days. What an experience.

Finally, the big Red Hat book signing day is here. There are a lot of Red Hat ladies here and they are all dressed up. Six red hatters from Fairview are here too. There are a lot of people who came by to find out more information about our group and what we do to have fun.

In the late afternoon, the girls packed everything up and then grabbed me from the window ledge and walked across the street to the Java Domain coffee shop. Wow, look at this place, it is all decorated with balloons. There is a big red hat balloon and one that says "It's your day" on it.

"What is happening here?" I asked.

"SURPRISE! HAPPY BIRTHDAY, SASSY!" All the girls shouted.

Happy Birthday

What a surprise! Jan explained that none of the other girls had a birthday in April. I was the only one, so everyone decided that we should celebrate my birthday. There is even a big cake with my picture on it. Oops, the cake says happy fifty-second birthday. I thought I was only fifty-one! There was even a beautiful birthday card that was signed by everyone and it says fifty-two on it. I must be fifty-two! The girls bought me a little light purple suitcase for a birthday present. Now I have something to keep my hats and other gifts in. There are Red Hat ladies here from Falher and Fairview too. Wow, they travelled all that way for this party.

A Purple Suitcase for All My Worldly Goods

There is a cute little dog here too. I had my picture taken with him as he sat on the big couch.

Rose arrived a little late and was wearing her work uniform because she came directly from work to my party. I wonder if any other mascots are treated like this. I feel so special and wanted by this great group of ladies. I am so emotional that a couple of little red and purple tears run down from my eyes. What a special day for me. I will never forget this love and celebration.

I am leaving to visit with Sally now. She took me to her car, opened the door and then opened the sunroof window.

"What are you doing to me?" I asked.

She giggled and said, "I've got a special surprise for you."

She picked me up, took my hat off and put it on the car seat, stuffed my head out of the sunroof and then closed the window around my neck so that I could not move. Boy, am I ever stuck up here, and my feet are dangling. The window is real tight against my throat, but I can still breathe.

"What are you doing?" I asked again.

Again, she just smiled and giggled. I never, ever had this done to me before. Sally brought her camera and took a picture of course, because most people would not believe that this happened to me. She got back in her car, started it up and then started driving. It was slow at first and then she drove faster and faster. At least it seemed that way. The wind makes my ears go straight out behind me and flap all over the place. It's a good thing that I do not have a hat on because it would go flying and I would never find it again. I am trying to keep my eyes open so I can see where we are going. There are people on the side-walk waving, pointing and giggling at me. One vehicle almost crashed into us. Sally had her car window open so she waved at them and smiled. People driving other vehicles honked their horns and waved at us. Boy, we are sure going to be the talk of the town tonight. We drove all over town and then finally got back to her place. I sure saw things that I never saw before! What a view!

How many times do you see a purple dog sticking out of the sunroof of a car? Only in Peace River with a Red Hat lady of course!

Another Adventure

Sally finally stopped the car, got out, loosened the window from my neck, and took me, my hat, and my new light purple suitcase into her house. What a car ride without a seat belt. I sure did not need one in that position. That wind was cold. Since our visit started out this way, I wonder what else she is planning. This will be quite the story to tell everyone at the next get together.

It has been a year now since Rose rescued me from boredom.

Let me remember … I met and visited with lots of the Sassy REDs ladies, attended lots of coffee nights, wore a seatbelt in many vehicles, travelled twice to Dunvegan, once in two black garbage bags stuffed in the truck of a car, learned to dance, watched a movie on a big screen, did fence sitting, attended a "reduation," became a flag person, learned how to wash and dry clothes, found Halloween to be fun, saw a lunar eclipse, wore a poppy on November 11, attended the Festival of Trees, got attacked by Casper the cat, visited Rose's coworkers, learned about Elvis, went to a luau, had fun in the park, learned about making cookies, got tipsy on wine, got inked, sat in the window of the bookstore, got a birthday cake and gifts, went shopping in stores and got my head stuck out of a car's sunroof. Wow, what a life I am living now. I wonder what will happen this next year.

Most of the things have been fun, and of course a few have not. Lately, it seems to me like the girls are all having a contest to see who can do the funniest things with me. Life is definitely not dull anymore.

Sally has lots of dolls. There are all shapes and sizes. She has this horse that goes up and down. It looks like fun. She set me on it and up and down I went. This is fun!

She then showed me a big white elephant.

"No, no, I do not to get on this elephant," I said.

"Sure you do; it will be fun," she said.

He looks friendly, so I agreed. This is the first time I ever rode on an elephant.

Sally put me on a big soft comfy chair, then brought over a little dog and set him on a little table next to me. She said that he is a mongrel and his name was "Red." She did something to the dog and suddenly he was singing. He sang "Only You." Several times a day I got to listen to him sing a love song to me. What a voice! I love listening to him. My heart just did a flip flop. I think that maybe I am falling in love. He was far away from me and I was sitting on the floor, so I wiggled a little closer.

"I am going to get a little closer to you, and a little closer, just a bit more," I said to him as I wiggled closer.

He is sitting on a little table singing away.

"Sing me more songs," I said.

And he did.

How do I love thee, let me count the ways. Oh, be still my heart. This must be love.

He leaned forward.

"Oh, Frank," I murmured.

Sassy in Love?

Sally said that she does not trust me to be alone with Red and that she wants to take me to her church. She explained that most people go to a big building, mostly on Sunday mornings, and listen to the word of God. It normally takes about an hour or so. We all have to sit quietly and listen to what is being said.

An hour? What happens if I have to, you know, GO? Then what? I would have to hold it? I have a tiny bladder. I do not think it would be a good idea for me to attend this service.

"Why can't I just stay here and listen to Red sing to me?" I asked.

"No, you do not know each other well enough to spend time unsupervised," she said.

She decided not to take me to the church service and had one of her dolls watch out for me while she was gone.

When Sally brought me to the next coffee meeting she explained that she thinks that I fell in love with her singing dog. She jokingly said that if I start to gain weight, there just might be a litter of purple and black puppies we would have to take care of too. Everyone giggled and said that it was a great idea to add that to my story.

Joy said that she wanted to take Sassy home with her this round. I wonder what she has planned for me. She carried me to the car, buckled me in and took me to her home. It sure is quiet here. She has a nice place and found a big pillow for me to sit on.

"Where am I going now?" I questioned.

It seems like I say that a lot, but I do a lot of travelling. Joy took me outside, and then I was put in the back seat of the car and we travelled for just a short time. There is a special meeting to learn how to take care of summer flower pots. Maybe I can grow my own flowers now. We go to a greenhouse, and the owner teaches us how to prune and take care of our potted flowers. What a learning experience. Some of the ladies actually bought flowers to take home with them.

Rose was there, and she drove me home. A few days later, she said that it was time to take me for a ride again. I wonder where she is going. I recognise this place. She is taking me back to that store where I got my cute purple hat. We went into the store together, and she found a red album to keep all the write-ups and pictures that she is keeping about my history of being a mascot for the Sassy REDs. She took me to the till with her. It was the same lady, and she remembered me! Rose paid for the album and then we went back to the car.

"Where are we going now, Rose?" I asked.

I was on the front seat, so I kept watching the road. Hey, I know where she is taking me. She is going to the place where she works. She did not even put me in a plastic bag this time; she just picked me up and carried me into the store. We found a big shopping cart and she put me in that little square section right in front so that I could see where I was going. We headed to the bakery department, and there I met the lady that does most of the cake decorating. Rose introduced me to Theresa. She smiled at me said that she loved my eyes and ears. She picked up the plate of cookies and offered me one, so I took a chocolate chip one. We talked with her for a bit, and then we went walking around the store. We met the main store manager, who is Rose's boss. I was introduced to him and he asked us to come to his office.

"Oh, oh, I wonder if you are in trouble because of the sign that says "No Dogs Allowed," I whispered to her. I sure am nervous about this meeting.

We followed him into his office. Rose put me on a little table and she sat down on a chair. He sat in his chair, looked back and forth at the both of us a couple of times, then giggled and said that it is sure true that pets and their owners look alike. I thanked him and then smiled. Rose explained to him about the Sassy REDs and me being their mascot and all the things that I do with the girls. He thought that it was quite the story, but I do not think that he believed everything she said. But that is the way it is with most people.

Rose said goodbye, he hugged both of us, and then we went to the till to pay for the things that she was buying. I got one little ride again. It sure is fun. We walked out the door, got in the car and went back home.

The Red Hat ladies ordered a big banner that we can use for functions. It is finally finished and it sure looks great. We are going to take it to a hot dog roast at Beth's place. She lives out of town so it will be nice and quiet there. There were a whole bunch of us in the car, but there was still room for me to sit on the back seat. No trunk ride this time, thank goodness! The ladies put up the banner for everyone to see. Everybody brought a different kind of food. That kind of a meal is called a potluck meal. There sure was lots of food. Beth owns a big place so we all walked around a lot. We even saw a train go by. What a fun time.

We all headed back to Peace River, and I stayed with Rose again.

The girls have been real busy planning for the "Big Bike Ride." Everyone has to collect money for the Heart and Stroke Foundation through pledges and then ride a huge red bike through town. The girls went around to their friends and got pledges and collected over $10,300. Wow, that is a lot of money. It was the highest amount in the area and the second highest amount in the whole province of Alberta. One lady raised $1,700 all by herself! The bike was so huge that we asked our husbands to help us ride. I think I even saw the mayor of Peace River who volunteered to help. The girls brought our new banner, and it was placed right in the front of the big bike.

There were two young men who were in charge of organizing the ride. Rose brought me and introduced me to them and asked if I could ride on the big bike. They giggled and said that yes, I could ride on the bike, but they had to find a safe spot just for me. One of the young men involved with the bike ride was named Martin. He looked at me, smiled and then tickled my nose. Yep, I like him too. They'd *never* been asked to have a mascot along for the ride. Because this has never happened to them before, they looked and looked for a place for me and then finally decided that I should sit right in front in the middle on a little pad. The organizers set me in that special place and buckled me in so that I would not fall off, especially going around corners.

They sure asked a lot of questions about me and even offered to take me with them to Yellowknife, a city north of Alberta, which was their next stop. All the girls thought that I should stay here in Peace River because they did not want me to get lost and not be able to find my way back home. It is a long, long way away. It sure is a hot day because there is a lot of blue sky up there and no clouds. The organizers had a little hose and they squirted water at everyone to cool all of us down. I even got some water drops on me.

Big Bike Ride

Okay, everybody, let's get on this huge bike and go for a ride around town. Everyone found a seat and then started to pedal. I could hear some people huffing and puffing when we had to go up a little hill and then relax a bit when we went down. We even had to stop at the traffic light because it had turned red when we got to it. It sure was interesting to try and go around sharp corners. What a long fun ride. We all sang the "B-I-N-G-O" song but said S-A-S-S-Y instead.

After the ride was over, we all got in our own vehicles and drove to Judy's place and had hot dogs and potato salad. The two young organizers were sure pleased. A whole bunch of awards were given out to everyone. It depended on how much your total pledge amount was as to what you received. I even got a cap and it fit just fine. I was so happy to be included.

There was a write-up in the local newspaper, and the ladies later received a plaque and thank you letter from the Heart and Stroke Foundation for all our efforts.

Some ladies heard that there are restaurant owners in town that are wondering why we are not going to their places for our coffee nights. It sounds like we are getting to be well known in Peace River. The ladies finally decided that we will find places to go other than Travellers. Su Casa is the first place that we visited. I got to sit in a special chair so that I could see everyone. It sure felt different being here instead of Travellers. I love to hear what the girls are planning and what is happening in their lives.

The manager of Travellers is retiring, so we planned to make a special visit there and wish him good luck. When the Sassy REDs first started, Queen Jan contacted John at the Travellers Hotel and told him about the group. He offered us a special big round table for our coffee nights. It was reserved just for us. He loved all the ladies and made sure that everything was perfect when we arrived. Six ladies got all dressed up in red and purple and attended John's retirement party. He sure was glad to see all of us and had pictures taken with us. He is planning to move to Edmonton.

John Vogt retirement

Rose is planning another Christmas in July, but she and her husband bought themselves a trailer and have been busy packing everything in boxes. Judy volunteered to have the party at her place. She has a nice big, shady backyard and Christmas ornaments on the fence. All the husbands came too. It was a great party. Rose made a dirt cake for dessert. It is made in a flower pot with real flowers stuck in it. The guys did the barbequing.

Christine decided to take me to her place because she wanted to have a couples barbecue. No stomach problems now with the big hill. It was a nice evening and she lit a fire in a big round steel pit. The guys really enjoyed the barbecue too. They were talking of maybe starting a men's group.

A bus load of ladies came from Falher for a special supper at TJ's, which is a Chinese restaurant. We booked the big back room so we would all be together. Everyone had to sit in a special place so that they had to talk to a stranger. The meal was super. We all wanted to get a picture taken, but there just was not enough room so we all walked across the street to the Riverdrive Mall parking lot and stood on a set of stairs. There were forty-three of us and we finally all fit! People coming out of the mall were sure surprised to see all the different red hats and purple outfits. A man even offered to take pictures for us. Several people asked who we were and what do we do. We are ladies over fifty who dress up and have fun. Rules? What rules? Just be at least fifty years old, dress in purple and wear a red hat.

It is getting close to the Festival of Trees again, and we are busy working on ideas. The girls have a tree that was donated by Rose. She and her husband want a new tree, possibly a white one, so that is why they gave this tree to the girls. The ladies were putting on all the sparkly lights. Someone said that there are 547 lights. Wow, that will be a bright tree when it is done. By the time the Festival of Trees is here, the ladies will have worked on the tree for three months.

There are some ladies in a small community called McLennan that invited us for supper. Judy volunteered to drive some of the girls there. Rose put me in the back seat, buckled me in and then we rode with Judy and Jan to that small town. There was a good turnout and everyone enjoyed the meal. Of course I was very careful this time and did not knock anything over. I just sat there and smiled at all the ladies. They were real curious about me so Rose explained how and where she found me but still kept her "little secret" about me.

I heard Rose talking to someone on the telephone. She has to work, but a train trip was mentioned. It is called the Northern Alberta Centennial Train Ride. A bunch of ladies are going to wear their Christmas tree skirts as capes, long dresses and red hats. It takes all day for the return trip. There is a luncheon at the halfway mark. The train stops on the way back and there are robbers on horses attacking the train and "robbing" people. All the money goes to a special organization. There is a bunch of shooting and all the robbers lie on the ground until the train leaves. It costs a lot of money to go, so that is why I have to stay with Rose again.

Jan is planning a Halloween party this year. I remember the little trick-or-treaters who came last year. There is a new lady here from a long, long way away. She is from Amsterdam. Her name is Fia; she is Betty's sister and is here for a visit. Jan phoned and asked Rose if she and I could get there early because Jan had a surprise for me. We went out the door to the car, and drove to Jan's place. When we got there, she showed me a huge pumpkin. She said that she wants to put me inside and put the lid back on it. Later on, she would surprise the ladies and show them where I am hiding. She picked me up and put me in the pumpkin. I did not quite fit, so she squished and turned me and I finally fit. Jan put the lid on the huge pumpkin and told me to wait and that I would be out soon. I agreed to do it because it is something new and sounds like fun. I can hear the ladies coming in. They are all excited. I kept real quiet.

Sometime during the evening Jan asked, "Has anyone seen Sassy?"

Everyone said, "No."

Jan walked over to the big pumpkin, lifted the lid and said, "Surprise, here she is."

I peeked out. Everyone clapped their hands. Jan picked me up and set me on a little chair.

There was great food. Some was orange and some was black. There was even a big frozen hand in the punch bowl. Jan's husband, Heinz, used his hand as the form. There were lots and lots of spiders all over the place too. Jan bought two identical puzzles. She put in a bunch of pieces and then the girls were divided into two groups and had to finish the puzzles. What a neat game. I went back home with Mascot Mum (Rose).

Rose and her husband are having a special turkey supper at their place in November. It is a special day in their religion. Lots of people come, and some are from other towns as far away as Grande Prairie. Rose introduced me to some of the ladies and guys. They thought I was cute. Some of the ladies heard of the

Red Hat Society so they are thinking of finding groups where they live. Rose's son, daughter-in-law and three grandsons came too.

Well, it is time again for the Festival of Trees. There are a lot of girls here to decorate the tree. I am going to sit and guard the tree again, just like I did last year. Rose put a red bandanna and tulle on me with a sign that said I was a mascot. It has been a long day, and I am kind of tired. I closed my eyes. I heard singing, music, and talking. I saw flashing and twinkling lights. I opened my eyes. I was having another great dream.

It is finally gala night. There are lots of people here again for the auction, and they are bidding on all the different items. Most of the items on our tree are homemade. There are little bonnets, gifts, pails, gingerbread girls, purple feathers and even wooden spoons. There is a red bird with a purple nest on the top of the tree. Our tree went up for auction like last year, and it sold for $600 this year. Rose's boss bought the tree and plans to put it in the store. Most of the bids were lower this year than they were last year. Rose put a little bid on a youth tree, and later she found out that she got the bid. It needed a little bit of help, so her husband fixed it.

I sat under the tree and watched everyone walk by. I smiled at them a lot and lots of people pointed at me like they did last year.

Festival of Trees

Well, the Festival of Trees is over again for another year. Rose came and picked me up and took me home.

I am staying with Rose because her party is in a few days. Her husband is busy putting wood on the bottom of the walls. It sure looks good. I sat with him and watched some TV. He likes NASCAR. Boy, do those cars ever travel fast, but they just go round and round in circles. There is a crash sometimes too. He also watches a show where these guys in a big ring hit and beat each other up. It is called wrestling. It looks painful. I enjoy watching TV. There are a lot of different shows to watch.

Rose put a hat on me, and she is dressed up to go somewhere. Judy picked us up and we are driving to Megan's place. She is planning a fashion show. There are a lot of big animals on the road when it gets dark, so she is driving slowly. There are nine Red Hat ladies here, and two neighbours of Megan's. They think we are a little odd because they have me as a mascot. As I said before, some people just do not understand about mascots.

"Hey, we do have a lot of fun and they are sure a busy group of ladies," I said.

Some of the ladies fashioned the clothes. They sure are nice outfits. It was a fun evening.

It is December and Rose is doing her annual Christmas party. Wow, there are seventeen ladies here; that broke that long-time, thirteen in attendance, spell. Rose has a decorated box on the floor to put the stocking stuffers in. There is another decorated box on the floor and it is covered with a green tablecloth.

She said, "NO PEEKING."

I wonder what she is up to. She put me on a little table by the Christmas tree. Rose made everyone a little corsage with purple velvet ribbon, a yellow flower and a green feather. She then handed out a little bag of goodies. A "count the candy" game was the first one; the second was a story of a little girl at Christmastime, and everyone got to pick a gift; next, was the hat contest. My green earmuffs with flowers on them were even included, and someone got to wear them too! The stocking stuffers this year were red and cost exactly $3.85. Rose handed out happy face stickers for people who spent the exact amount and sad faces for those who did not. When the gifts were opened, each lady had to admit to buying them and tell how much they spent.

Oh, Oh, red panties with feathers on them. Everyone giggled and got excited and wondered who did that? No one wanted to confess. Finally, Heather confessed that she was the one. What a hoot. There is lots of food of shrimp, sliced meats, fresh veggies and a bunch of squares.

I am staying with Rose for a few more days. Here we go again. Back up to where she works. She needed to buy a few things. I rode in the shopping cart again, and then I met another lady that works at the bakery. No, I did not get a cookie today because they were all gone. We walked around the store for a long time and several people stopped and talked to us. We finally went to the till, and I got to go on a couple more rides.

It is coffee night again so I jumped in the front seat of the car with Rose and away we went. My little seat was waiting for me. A man named George came over to talk to us ladies and he asked about me. They explained that I am a mascot and that I love my job. He said that he had a little gift for me. He brought out this little flashy champagne glass necklace and put it over my head for me to wear.

"Oh, thank you so very much," I said.

Well, the end of the year is here again. What a year it has been! I wonder what is in store for me next year.

CHAPTER 6

It is now January again, a brand new year, and we are having our first coffee at Travellers. There are fourteen ladies here. Our group sure has grown this past year. The girls were talking about plans for the next couple of months. Some of the girls are excited about having me visit them. There are so many now that not everyone can have me for a long visit. They are chatting about different things to do with me.

"Oh, oh! It sounds like I am going to be up to my neck in hot water," I whispered.

The girls giggled and then smiled. It is *really* becoming a contest now of who can come up with real unique things for me to do. I have done lots of things and some have been not so nice. Again, I wonder if any other mascots are doing this or if they just sit and wait for a big major event to attend.

Phyllis is going to be fifty real soon so the girls are planning a "reduation" for her. We decided that we will hold it at Travellers. I am going home with Rose until the party.

Rose is all dressed up in a nice purple outfit and a fancy big hat. She put a little hat on me and we went out the door to the car and drove to the reduation for Phyllis. There are fifteen ladies here. Wow! What a turnout. One of the ladies made a red hat cake for the event. After everyone arrived, Jan said a little speech about Phyllis joining our group and placed a special red hat on her head. She is now officially a "Red Hatter." Everyone clapped their hands and hugged her, including me. She got to cut the cake. It was delicious. When the party was picked me up and I went back to her place.

Joyce planned a movie night for the girls. Nine ladies a here. She put the movie in the machine but was having problems with getting the movie to come on the television screen. She finally figured out how to make the machine work, and we sat and watched *Shall We Dance*. After the movie, she made an announcement about birthdays. She decided that tonight it will be everybody's birthday. We all sang happy birthday to each other.

I stayed with Joyce until the next coffee meeting. Her husband is still not noticing me that much, but he did smile at me and then waved. It's working. I am getting to him.

More new ladies! It seems like every time there is a coffee night, there are new faces. We might need a bigger place to hold our coffee nights. After the coffee, the girls were talking about who would take me home with them. Myrna won, so I am going to visit her. She told the girls that she was going to have some fun with me. Here we go again, I wonder what she is up to.

She carried me outside and buckled me in the front seat of her car. She lives right in town, so it was not a far drive to her place. It is a huge building. She called it an apartment building. There is a funny panel at the door so that you can buzz all the residents who live there. She took out her key, opened the big door and then we went to her apartment.

She set me on her kitchen table and then sat down on a chair, looked at me and smiled. She had a big smile and she really looked at me for a long time. I just knew that she was up to no good. She said that she was thirsty, stood up, went into the fridge and took out a can. She then went to a cupboard, opened it and took out a glass. She put the glass on the table and then opened the can. She poured half of the liquid into the glass. It was amber coloured and foamy. She then set the can and the glass that was half full of the drink in front of me, laid me on my side and took a picture of me with this half empty can and glass. This has never happened to me before.

"What is in the can and the glass?" I asked.

"It is an alcoholic drink called beer," she explained. "I want the girls to think that you and I had a drink together before going to bed. I laid you on your side so that it looks like you had too much to drink, got a little tipsy and fell over."

"That's funny," I said, giggling. Memories flooded back from the special supper when I drank wine.

Me and Beer

I wondered if the girls would realize that Myrna was just having fun with me. She drank all the beer and then she took me with her to the bedroom and set me on a chair. She crawled into bed and went to sleep. I closed my eyes and went to sleep too.

Here I go again. It is coffee night, and, boy, wait until the girls find out what Myrna and I did. There are thirteen ladies here, and they all giggled about the picture, the beer and me lying on my side on the table. They all thought it was a fun thing to do to me. I am wondering if all this fun is really getting out of hand. Again, it seems like it is a fun contest about what the ladies can do to me and get away with.

Jan wants to take me to her place again. I had fun with her husband, Heinz, the last time I stayed with her. Away we went to Jan's place. Heinz was doing something on the computer when we got there.

"Hello, Heinz," I said. He smiled and winked at me.

Jan is busy so I stayed in the computer room with him. He set me on a chair beside him. I sat and watched him do accounting. Boy, there are sure lots of numbers. He then went on the internet for some information. Are there ever a lot of things on the Net! That is what he called it. When he got done with that, he and I sat at the table and played a card game. He called it solitaire. It sure looks like a fun game. He explained a lot of things to me that night. It was a little confusing at times, but it was enjoyable. I spent the next couple of days learning about the computer from Heinz. He is a good teacher.

It is coffee night again, and Jan is dressed in purple and looking for a simple hat to wear.

"Can I go too?" I asked.

"No, not tonight," Jan said.

She explained that there is a special event that she wants to take me to next week. I will have more fun at this new event instead of just going for coffee. I stayed home and played solitaire again with Heinz. He said that he likes my company.

Jan was telling me that there is a "Baroque and Beyond" event which is an evening of seventeenth- and eighteenth-century music theatre and art. She is all dressed in a Christmas tree skirt and put on a cape too. She put a special hat on me and my little red boa. Judy, Jan and Christine even wore small

Victorian hats that Judy made. The hats were made from a thin plastic cutting board. Judy drove and picked up me and Jan. We waited outside of the building until the rest of the girls arrived, and then we all walked in together. Because of the way we were dressed, many of the people there thought that we were part of the production. I sat with the girls and really enjoyed the show. Several people came over to the table and talked to the ladies. Jan explained that I was their mascot. What a beautiful evening.

Jan is sure on the phone a lot, talking to some of the ladies about the special invitation that we got to go to Fairview. The Sassy REDs have been invited by the Fairview Sew & So's to go to Fairview for a celebration.

Finally, the day has arrived to go to Fairview. Jan sure does not look good. She is wheezing and coughing. Her eyes are looking red too.

"Hey, Jan, if you are not well enough to go, how will I get there?" I asked.

Jan said that she contacted Sue, who is one of our newest members, about picking me up.

"Oh boy, oh boy, I can go!" I said.

Sue finally arrived, got out of the car and came to the door. Jan put a special hat on me. When Sue arrived at the door, Jan picked me up and handed me to Sue and reminded her to make sure that I had the seat belt on. Sue took me to her car, opened the front door, put me on the seat and buckled me in. She got in, started the car and drove to a small town called Grimshaw. We were supposed to meet some ladies here and then travel together. Nope, they are not here, so we started driving again to Fairview.

We found the place for the celebration. Sue found a parking spot, and we went into the building. Wow, look at all the ladies here for this special event. We all signed in and got name tags. I got one too. We were assigned tables based on the month of our birthday. I was allowed to sit with Rose at her table, even though her birthday is in May and mine is in April.

Introductions were made and a poem called "Warning" was read. It is the official Red Hat poem. Lunch was a variety of meats, vegetables, fruits and squares. There was coffee, tea and juice. There was a special cake for the occasion too. There was also a big red hat and a pair of red boots for decoration. A skit was performed with the poem "Ode to the Old Lady in the Mirror." Kenny Rogerstein and Dolly Pardonable made a special appearance and sang "Islands in the Stream."

There was a leafless tree with shoes on it and a poem called "Grandma's Shoes" was recited with another lady pointing out the shoes.

The special "celebration" was finally going to happen! There was a big purple box on a ledge. A lady explained that in the box was a very special person. Another lady opened the box and lifted out a beautiful white teddy bear with dangly legs, a cute nose, a red hat and a purple scarf. This was going to be the Red Hat Sew and So's mascot.

"A mascot! Wow! I get to meet ANOTHER Mascot!! I am going to visit with my first mascot!" I said excitedly.

The lady had a special wand and christened her Scarlett O'Hatta. I was so excited. My ears went up and down, and I even jumped a couple of times. My hat even lifted off my head twice. The lady pressed a little button on the teddy's paw and she sang "Girl's Just Want to Have Fun." What a beautiful voice. I hope that she will have just as much fun as I do. Boy, could I ever tell her some stories, good and bad, of what has happened to me. We even had our picture taken together.

A lot more pictures were taken and then everyone headed back home. Rose and I went back with Sue. I am going back home with Rose until the next coffee night. Sue dropped us off, and we went into the house. Both of us were real tired. What a great evening.

The next day, Rose's husband, Burt, saw me and welcomed me back. I have been visiting a lot and he sort of missed me. It is Monday and he likes to watch wrestling in the evening. There is a friend of his with him. His name is Dave. I was introduced to him, and he looked at me kind of funny. Men usually do; they just do not understand the attraction of some mascots.

It is time for Wednesday night coffee. Rose pinned a funny looking hat on me and away we went to Travellers. We were sure surprised to see so many ladies here. Our group sure is growing by leaps and bounds. There are two new girls here tonight. They thought I was adorable sitting in my little chair. The ladies are discussing plans for a larger place for our coffee nights and the international supper that we hold once a year. They are planning some entertainment. Sounds like there will be a few surprises too. The girls decided that I should be able to sign in at events like all the other girls do. They are going to order me some little black paw prints. Lately Rose had been drawing a little paw print to show everyone that I am attending events.

"Whom am I going home with tonight?" I asked.

I am going back to be with Jan again for a while. She reminded me that my birthday is coming real soon. Even with all the new girls that have joined our group, I am still the only one who has a birthday in April.

Jan is all dress up again and is wearing a big red hat. She put a hat on my head and stuck some pins in it.

"Where are we going now, Jan?" I asked.

She said that a bunch of ladies are getting together at TJ's Restaurant for a meal. We jumped into her car and headed for the restaurant. We opened the door and walked in. We walked to the big back room and, wow, there are a lot of ladies here. Someone said that there are thirty-six of us. Look at the sea of red and purple. The Buzzing Red Hats from Smokey River are here too. I remember them from last year when they all came in a bus. They did that now too. I looked and looked but could not see their mascot. Maybe they just forgot to bring her. I know what that is like because the Sassy REDs still forget about me sometimes.

The buffet was great, and there were lots of different kinds of food. The ladies were trading places all night so they could talk to other people. There were even two pink hatters there too. Pictures of the different tables were taken but not a group picture because there were too many and there just was not enough room. When the girls were walking out and paying their bills, I heard a lot of people in the main part of the restaurant talking about the huge lineup of red and purple that seemed to never end. A lot of them were wondered about what was going on and who we were. A few asked Rose about the group of ladies. Yep, the news about the Sassy REDs is sure getting around town.

A bunch of the ladies went to a play by the Peace Players Production called *Sorry about This.*

I went back to Jan's place again. The next day, I saw Jan digging some things out of her closet and sorting them. She mumbles something about sorting things because she wants to retire soon and move away from Peace River.

"Jan, am I hearing this right? Are you going to move? Yikes! Move away from Peace River?" I asked.

She just looked at me, smiled and I saw a tear running down her cheek. She came over to me, picked me up and gave me a great big hug and then put me back down. I guess that means that we will not be visiting and seeing each other for a long time. Boy, will I ever miss her, as will all the rest of the girls. She helped the girls from Falher, Grimshaw and Fairview start up their groups. I guess that we will just have to wait and see what is going to happen.

Rose stopped by the next day to discuss the international supper. She took me home with her.

Rose put my purple hat on me and said that we had to go to the bakery where she works. I wonder what kind of cookie I will get this time. I do not have to worry anymore about that "No Dogs Allowed" sign. We got to the store, walked in, found a cart and then headed to the bakery. Rose asked Theresa about the cake for me.

"A cake! A cake like last year," I exclaimed.

I was so surprised. I was introduced to Mary, the new employee who brought out my cake from the big cooler. It looked great. Mary and Theresa both giggled that the cake was for me. We went to the till and paid for the cake. I even got my little ride. We then left the bakery and went back home.

Later, Rose picked me up and we went to the car, buckled in and drove to Travellers for the party. There were lots of ladies again. They sat me in my little chair and put the cake in front of me. They had two candles on it, which they lit. Everyone sang "Happy Birthday" to me. I tried to blow out the candles, but it just did not work so Rose and Jan did it for me. Of course I got gifts again. These ladies sure buy me a lot of nice things. There was a red purse, a new hat and some pens. What a party. These girls sure do know how to have fun. What a year again. I went to a reduation, rode the big bike, fell in love with a cute dog, met another mascot, went to Baroque and Beyond, attended lots of coffee nights, attended a fashion show, posed for a picture where I looked drunk, attended Rose's Christmas in July and of course the Festival of trees. What a year!

It is time again for the international supper at Travellers. I got dressed up in my birthday hat and boa. The place is so nicely decorated. I am not going to have anything to drink tonight, for sure. There are a lot of ladies here. It is an ocean of red and purple. The Red Hat ladies from Falher, Fairview and

Grimshaw are here to. The food was superb, and the highlight of the evening was an Elvis singer who sang a song. What a night to remember.

It is all over the news that a black bear strolled into the store where Rose works, walked to the bakery, sat in the cake department and ate some cake. It was late at night so there was no one in the bakery at the time. A store employee saw the bear and it was led back outside. The bear got in because the doors to get into the store automatically open when you get close to them. At work the next day, Rose brought one of her teddy bears and put it where the bear sat.

Well, another reduation. Tina has been a pink hatter for a lot of years, and she is finally allowed to wear a red hat and purple clothes because she is now fifty years old. She collects teddy bears, so the girls decided to have a "teddy bear picnic" for her reduation. Judy and Jan were talking about a special hat for her to wear. Judy quickly rushed to town, rushed home, snipped off the ears of a teddy bear and created a special teddy hat for her. The party was held at Tina's place. Wow, there are twenty ladies here. They were told to bring teddy bears for the event. The house was full of them. They were on the furniture, on the floor, hanging from lamps and sitting on the windowsills. Look at all the bears. Rose had a homemade pattern for a bear skin rug, so she made one as a gift. There was even a teddy bear cake, the only edible teddy in the house. The final count was 146 teddy bears! Jan congratulated Tina and placed a special teddy hat on her head.

I am going to stay here for a visit. A few days later, Betty picked me up and said that I was going to attend something special. She put me in her car, buckled me in and away we drove up the hill to the store where Rose works. Betty said that it was Rose's birthday, and we were going to surprise her with a birthday party. She contacted the store and found out when Rose's lunch break was. Betty even brought a purple hat for Rose to wear.

Rose was sure surprised when she walked in the lunch room and we all shouted "Happy Birthday, Rose!"

The girls bought her a red rose in a little vase with a balloon attached to it as a gift. Rose's boss even put it over the PA system and told everyone to walk to the bakery and say happy birthday to her. She had a lot of visitors that day.

The bakery staff agreed that I could stay in the bakery until Rose went home as long as I was good and did not get in the way. They found a place at the front, right next to some beautifully decorated cakes, for me to sit and watch all the customers. Boy, did the guys who do the baking ever ask a lot of questions about me. They did not want me too close to them because they use a lot of flour and did not want me to get covered with it. They even mentioned that maybe they could kidnap me and then I would really have a story to tell everyone. They were thinking up about a whole bunch of bad things like throwing me on the side of the road, hanging me from a tree and even asking for a ransom to get me back.

Sassy at the Bakery

"Yipes, that does not sound like fun," I muttered.

I stayed in the bakery and watched Rose work and smiled at all the customers. When Rose got off work, she picked me up and we drove home. It sure feels good to be home again for a while.

A new lady named Coral lives at the manse at the Anglican Church and invited the girls for coffee. We got there and took a tour of the building. What a beautiful place. Most of us sat outside because it was a sunny day. There is a special grave site on the property too. Coral is having a yard sale so the girls have the first chance to purchase items.

There sure are a lot of girls who are having coffee parties at their home. I do miss some of them, but I really try to attend as many parties as I can.

I went to visit Joyce again for a while. Joyce is running around getting things organized for a special coffee party. She has been working on a new verandah for her house for a long time now. It is finally finished so she wants to show it to the girls.

All the girls are here, and it is sure warm sitting on her new porch. We all had juice, coffee and tea to drink and even some little snacks and squares. Rose took me home with her. It sure has been a busy summer.

Rose put a cute hat on me and away we went out to the car.

"Another party huh, Rose," I said.

She told me that it is Ellen's birthday, and she wanted to celebrate with us girls. She lives out in the country. It was a long trip. It was a pot luck meal. That means everyone brings a little something to eat. After lunch, Ellen showed us her studio. Ellen is an artist and she does mushroom art. She sets the mushrooms on special paper overnight and the spores from the mushroom stay on the paper. Different mushrooms make different designs. It was very informative. The property is quite large so a lot of the ladies decided to walk around and enjoy the view.

"Hey, what about me" I asked. "Can I come too? Hey! *Yoo-hoo*!" I yelled.

Nope, they did not hear me. Finally they came back. I heard someone mention that when they took pictures I was too far away, so they did not have time to come back and get me. It was another fun outing. Boy, there sure have been lots of them.

Tina took me home. I am going to visit with her until Rose's annual Christmas in July party. We got to Tina's place and her grandson Joey was so happy to see me. Her other grandson Phil was in bed, so I stopped in and saw him too. I even spent the night with him. The next morning, I sat and listened while Tina read a book to the boys. I then sat and watched the boys play a video game.

Tina put a new hat on me. That must mean that we are going somewhere. She and the boys were heading into town, so they took me too. They left me in the car to be a watch dog. I did it very well. I even met the boys other grandparents. They really liked me, and we had a good visit.

We got back to Tina's place and the boys took me outside and showed me the tent that they set up so they could sleep in it. I have not been in a tent before so I took a peek inside. There were sleeping bags in there.

"Hey, boys, can I sleep in here with you?" I asked.

"Of course," they both answered.

I slept in the tent for two nights with the boys. It sure got cool in the evening, but the boys cuddled me and kept me warm.

The next day, Tina took the boys to a circus. They left me at home because of that money thing again.

When no one was looking, Phil picked me up and snuck me out side. From the way he was looking around, I knew that I was in trouble.

"What are you going to do to me?" I questioned.

No answer. He kept walking around the yard and then went over to a big tree. He reached up and stuck me on a big branch and then ran away and just left me hanging there.

"Help! Help! Somebody help me out of this tree!" I yelled. "I am stuck here and cannot get down!"

Finally, I saw Joey come out of the house.

"Help!" I screamed again.

He heard me and came running over, rescued me from the tree and took me back into the house. This is another new adventure for me.

Tina is having a Red Hatter breakfast. All the food is blue themed, like blueberry muffins. She has blue plates and napkins too. She held the breakfast outside on her patio. Four ladies arrived for this fun event. I did not have coffee but the juice was sure good.

Well it is time again for Rose's annual Christmas in July party. Tina and I drove up to Rose's place and, wow, look at all the Christmas decorations! She must have spent a lot of time doing this. There are snowmen and candy canes on the fence, a whole bunch of big red Christmas stockings on her clothesline, hats all over the fence and even ninety-two balloons. Rose also had a huge, four-foot-tall, stuffed snowman in her yard. She said that a lot of cars drove close to her place all day looking at the decorations and wondered what was happening. Her neighbours even came over and talked to her. She really has gone overboard for this party. No wonder all the girls love coming to her parties.

The event is going to be held outside because the weather is real nice. We all went to the shady part of her yard that she had decorated for the party. There are fourteen ladies here and everyone is real excited. Rose did a "candy in the jar" count again. Everyone had to put their guesses into a special draw box.

It was a huge black and purple shoe. It was really a piñata that she painted purple and made into a draw box. What a fantastic idea. There were 198 candies, and Cora won the guess and the candies. Rose handed out little shaking snow ornaments and purple ribbon corsages for everyone.

She brought out a big box and said that there was a surprise inside. She had a list of things that might be found in a woman's purse. She called out an item and if one of the ladies could find the item in their purse, they got to take off one layer of wrapping paper. There were about thirty-three layers of wrapping and several different sized boxes. The final winner was Rita who got a little red letter holder with an envelope attached to it. In the envelope were two scratch-and-win Christmas lottery tickets. She scratched them and won two dollars. It was a real fun game, and the ladies want to do it again at her annual December Christmas party.

There was a hat contest, just like at the last party. Everyone wore a hat, and so did I. The winner was Betty with a hat that had a little angel on it.

It started to rain, so all the girls ran into the house for the rest of the party. The gift exchange was next on the agenda. There was a real variety of gifts again this year and Betty got the "gag" gift of a white pair of panties.

Luncheon included some green, pink, blue and purple bread sandwiches. The bread was made at the bakery where Rose works. She bought some and kept it in the freezer until this event. No one had ever seen anything like this. There was also a "kitty litter" cake. It tasted good according to the girls.

After lunch everyone was talking about Rose's annual December Christmas party. Instead of having a gift exchange, the ladies decided they would each buy a toy for a child and then donate the toys to the Salvation Army in time for Christmas. The cost will be $4.25 and the colour will be yellow. It will be a pot luck supper. That way Rose does not have to supply and pay for all the food herself. Everyone took home one of the stockings that Rose had on her clothes line. Everyone is to decorate them and bring them to the Christmas party, and then we will donate them to the Salvation Army too.

What a great party. Rose informed all the girls that her granddaughter has not been born yet, but it will happen real soon.

I am going home with Sue. I wonder what the next fun event will be.

Chapter 7

Sue told me that there is a supper tonight at TJ's. She has on a cute T-shirt and little hat. We jumped in the car and drove to the restaurant. We walked in and joined the other ladies. There were fourteen of us; again, a good head count.

Rose announced that she is a grandma to a little baby girl named Bailey. She has bad breathing problems, and when she was twelve-hours old she was air lifted from Grande Prairie to Stollery hospital in Edmonton. She will be having surgery very soon.

Well, it is official. Jan is retiring and is planning to move to the Okanagan in British Columbia. We are all going to miss her. She was the one who started this fun group of ladies. The girls are talking of some plans for a going away party for her. She will be leaving sometime in October or November, so we do have some time to plan a farewell party and invite the girls from Falher, Grimshaw and Fairview.

I am going back to visit with Sue because she is planning a fiesta night. Sue told me that I am to watch the house while she works.

"Okay, that works for me," I said.

Every day she would place me in a different room in her house. I liked that. Sue has a visitor, named Carmen, who is here from Nova Scotia now. Nova Scotia is far, far away on the other side of Canada. Carmen told me that she has a cat named Sassy. That's cool. I like that.

Sue is busy planning for her fiesta night. She is making all kinds of spicy food and real special drinks. She places chairs all over the house for the ladies to sit on. Decorations include a piñata, a huge hat and a guitar. Sue found a special chair for me to sit in. She even made a little sombrero hat for me to wear. Most of the ladies dressed up in fancy outfits for the evening. We played two games. One was making up a story and the other was a question and answer sheet about Mexican ideas. Everyone wrote down their names and then there was a draw for some door prizes.

Well the party is over. Sure was a fun time again. I wonder who will take me home this time. Nope, no one volunteered so I guess I will stay here and visit some more. Carmen and I had long talks about what it is like to live in Nova Scotia. She said that she does not belong to any Red Hat group, but now that she has had so much fun here, she just might consider joining.

I hear someone knocking at the door. It's Rose. She came back to pay for her hat that she picked out. She said that she will take me home now. I gave Carmen a big hug and told her that I really enjoyed our chats.

Rose is sure busy this morning getting ready for work. She found a cute red hat and put it on my head. She said that she had a surprise for me. She carried me out to the car, opened the door, buckled me on the front seat and drove to IGA.

She said that she made arrangements with the main boss and the bakery boss so that I can visit all day at the store. This sounds like fun.

The first people I met were the three bakers. They work at a big table making bread and buns. Les smiled at me and Steward looked at me kind of funny. Mary thought I was cute. I just winked and smiled at them. Rose explained who I was and said it was okay for me to be here. She put me on a little pedestal so that I could see everyone coming and going. I watched people pick up a variety of sweet food to take home.

Another coworker showed up. She sure got excited when she met me. Her eyes got as big as mine. She asked Rose about me, so she explained about finding me at a yard sale. Next was a young part-time student. She makes donuts and helps with the packaging.

Rose made and decorated three cakes and even made some strawberry shortcakes. They sure sold fast. Rose took me with her when she went on her lunch break. A lot of people asked her about me.

At the end of her shift, Rose put me in a shopping cart because she had to pick up a few things for supper. A little girl got real excited when she saw me. She squealed, so her mom asked about me. Several other people giggled when they saw me. How often do you see a purple dog in a shopping cart?

It sure was a fun day, and I learned about what Rose does at her job.

She is feeling a little sick and is sure walking slowly. She booked an appointment to see the doctor. He gave her a note to give her boss saying that she cannot work for a couple of days.

Rose is having problems with her hands. It has something to do with the meds she is on. Once she changed pills, the pain went away.

Well, coffee time again. Joanne is taking me to her place this time. She is driving really slow. There is a washout on the road, and there is a barrier to drive around. There is a sign that says the speed limit is ten kilometres. That is sure slow. Yikes, this is not a good situation. There are even boards on the road.

Finally we get to her place. She has a dog with one blue eye and one brown eye. He is on a chain outside. He looked at me kind of funny. I was introduced to her husband. He smiled at me and looked at me kind of funny too. That is quite normal for husbands.

I went to work with Joanne the next day. She works at the women's shelter. It is a building where women go to get help from being in bad situations and have no other place to turn for help. I sat on a shelf in the office. I met a lady and her son. I went to work with her every day. What an experience!

Joanne took me to a campground called Lac Cardinal. It is a real nice place with a whole bunch of trees. I stayed in the car a lot because of the smoke from the campfire and so I did not get wet when it rained real hard.

Well, my visit is over. It was sure different.

Judy will be sixty years old pretty soon and is planning a party at the Legion. She wants to invite all the Red Hatters, other friends and some relatives. The real surprise is that her husband is planning a party for Judy a week earlier. Judy has no idea that this is happening. We are all keeping this a big secret. Every time she makes a phone call to order cake decorations or food, her husband then phones and cancels it without her knowing.

It is time to surprise Judy. Burt, Rose and I drove to her place. We knocked on the door and she invited us in. She was a little surprised but did not say anything. Pretty soon more and more people came in. She finally figured out what her husband did to her. Everyone there wished her a happy sixtieth birthday. She wanted special name tags for everyone. She asked us to think of a friend or relative of hers that we could pretend to be. Rose said she was Judy's twin sister! I was her favourite toy as a child. There was a house full of people and we all munched, had drinks, talked, joked and finally went home.

Rose is putting a little hat on me again. That must mean that we are going out again. We got in the car and headed downtown to a restaurant. We got out of the car and walked into the café. There was a big table that we all sat around. There are fourteen of us here, including me. I got to sit in my favourite little chair. There are a couple of guys here who I think recognize me. They are waving and smiling, so I smiled back and wiggled my tail. All of us ordered our meals and then waited a long time to get the food. The girls were saying that it had taken over an hour already for our food to come. One lady was on her lunch hour and could not wait so she had to leave early.

When Rose's order came to her, it had a lot of mushrooms in it. She has a bad allergy to mushrooms and told the waitress about it, but it still came with them in it. She had to wait a long time again and then was charged half price for the one that was sent back. Betty even had to pay for a glass of lemonade and a tea that someone else had ordered and did not pay for. The ladies were not pleased and decided that they would not come back to this restaurant.

I am going back home with Rose again. It seems now that no one is interested in taking me home right now. Maybe they are getting bored or frustrated with coming up with things for me to do. Right now everyone seems to be real busy, too, with all the events going on and Christmas coming soon. Maybe something is being planned for me that everyone wants to keep secret. I guess that I just have to be patient and wait and see what will happen.

The ladies have been planning a goodbye for Jan for some time. That night is finally here. Everyone is to bring their boas, so I am taking mine too. Rose is dressed up in a nice dress and a big fancy hat. We got in the car and drove to the Senior's Centre. The room is nice and big, and we have lots of decorations and even a special cake sitting on a little table. There is that ocean of red and purple again. Everyone signed a special book that will be given to Jan at the end of the evening. There are ladies here from Falher, Grimshaw, Fairview and of course Peace River. I tried to count, but everyone was moving around and it got confusing. After everyone sat down, I counted and there were fifty ladies.

Queen Judy

Judy went and picked up Jan and they walked in the building. Jan walked under all the boas that the ladies were holding up. The song "Pretty Woman" was playing. Jan was so emotional that she started crying. Special gifts were presented to her. Jan said her goodbyes, and then she presented Judy with a new crown and scepter, making her our new queen. Joyce and Sue presented her with a new cape. There were several skits and a great meal. After all the entertainment, Jan cut the special cake and everyone had a piece of it. I sat with Scarlett O'Hatta, the mascot from Fairview. What a very emotional evening for everyone. I sure am going to miss her. I went home with Rose again.

I heard the phone ring. Rose was talking to Jan about me visiting with her one last time before she moves. I loved the idea. Rose put a special hat on me, picked me up, carried me to the car and away we drove to see Jan.

Jan opened the door and grabbed me and gave me a big hug. There were tears in her eyes. She and Rose visited for a while and talked about the changes that will be happening with the Sassy REDs now that she is moving.

Jan took me with her into her dressing room and explained that this is her last day of work in the government building. She wants to take me with her.

"What a great idea," I said.

She picked me up, buckled me into the front seat and away we went to where she works. Boy, it sure is a big building. We went through some doors and up some stairs and down some hallways and finally got to her office. She found a place for me to sit, and I watched her work. Her coworkers and boss came to visit with her. They all said how much they will miss her. I know the feeling. Jan even took a picture of me that day. It sure was an emotional day. She handed over her office key and we slowly left the building. She sure looks sad. She hugged me, which made both of us feel better.

At Jan's Workplace

It's coffee time again. The girls were talking about ideas for the Festival of Trees this year. They did not want to do a Christmas tree this year. Rose walked into a store and found this real nice looking huge metal wheel. She brought it up to the girls, and they agreed that we could turn it into a window scene. Rose volunteered her place this year to work on the project.

There have been several meetings for working on the wheel. We are going to add some little lights and a big red and white ribbon to it too. Burt is even helping with this project. Rose found a winter scene blanket that we will be using for the backdrop. We added a couple of little snowmen and some white stuff to make it look like fluffy snow. We talked about it for a long time at the coffee night. There are just finishing touches to put on it now, and then it will be done for the Festival of Trees.

No one wants to take me home with them, so Rose is picking me up and taking me back to her place. I wonder what is happening to the girls. They are acting so different to me now. Perhaps I am just imagining it, but I can sense that something is not quite right. Maybe I will have some excitement at the Festival of Trees gala. I sure had fun this past two years. There is usually a lot going on for those couple of days.

The girls are saying that the cost of the tickets for the gala night is a lot more than last year. Maybe this will be the last time that we attend. There have been changes with the event too.

The final touches have been made to the wheel, so Joyce will be picking up me and the wheel and taking us to the Travellers ballroom to set up the display. Rose is working, so she will not be helping this year.

"Hi, Joyce," I said when she came to pick me up. "I am all excited again this year."

She put me and the wheel into the car and then we drove to Travellers. Several of the girls were there to help set up the wheel. Judy bought two little red poinsettia plants to go with the wheel. They set me down in front of the wheel.

Guarding Wheel

"Goodbye, girls. I will see you all on opening gala night," I said.

Finally gala night is here again. All the girls are dressed up in their fancy outfits. It is like another sea of red and purple. Our wheel did not go up for auction, so it will just go to the highest bidder at the end of the event. The girls are a little disappointed, but we are still pleased with how it looked. Well, I think I will take a little nap.

CHAPTER 8

Where am I? I hear voices. What a horrible dream—it's more like a nightmare. The last thing I remember, I was at the Festival of Trees. I am all by myself now.

"Where are Rose, Judy, and the other ladies?" I asked.

I have something over my eyes so that I cannot see anything. I can hear talking. Someone said that I disappeared and no one knows where I am. Rose thought maybe a little girl loved me, picked me up and took me home by accident. I heard the talkers say that she contacted the radio station to report that I was missing. There are rumors about me being kidnapped all over the town of Peace River. Is being kidnapped what is happening to me right now? It sure is not a very nice feeling.

One day is feels like a week to me. I do not know how many days or weeks have gone by. I can hear voices again. The talk is about a coffee night and the girls asking about me. Someone delivered a letter to Rose when the girls all went out for supper at the Sunflower Café. The letter said that I was lonely and wanted an adventure.

Here is what the letter said:

Mum,

I am so sorry I left the Festival of Trees on my own. It was dark that Sunday night after the ladies had decorated the wheel, and it was so dark I started to get afraid again. This was the third time you had left me in that big scary building all alone.

"What the H—," I said. "I am not staying here by myself anymore in the dark."

I went upstairs through a smelly place. The people there are really frightening with coloured hair and metal all through their body parts. They were drinking a frothy drink that really smelled! I almost went back but bravely decided if I wanted an adventure, I had to have a little more courage.

Did you know, Mum, that around the corner from where we have coffee sometimes there are lots of machines with funny lights? Some of them even ring real loud and give the people there round metal disks. They get real excited when this happens. I decided to try one of the machines out. It seems you have to have some of those disks to start with though. (There is a picture of me sitting on a chair in front of the machine.)

I decided to go outside for a while to get away from all that smoky smell and found myself at this place where they keep dogs and cats. I think they treat them really well there because when I looked out the window, I could see people who were cleaning these little metal boxes out and putting in lots of warm blankets. There were big bowls of food in each metal box too! Suddenly, one of the ladies saw me looking through the window and gave a shout. Seems she thought I had gotten out of one of those metal boxes, and they started after me. It was a close call, I can tell you, as I got my collar caught on a hook on the fence. I heard later they put down lots of animals from there! I'm sure glad I managed to wiggle free in time. (There is another picture with me on a fence with a sign that says: Please do not feed, tease or touch the dogs.)

On the Fence

There were people going into the building down the street, so I rushed inside to hide for a while. Did you know that you can get money here too? Only it seems this time you need little pieces of paper to mark with these wonderful coloured pens! I tried to get one of them, but suddenly I was on a table with these pens, and I thought they were going to cover me in red and blue ink!! (Again, there is another picture of me in Bingo Hall.)

I thought I'd better get out of there real quick so, fast as I could, I ran back to the Festival of Trees where at least I knew I wasn't going to be as afraid as I was at this moment. Seems my sense of direction failed me when I needed it most. You have pampered me so much, Mum, that I couldn't find my way back and ended up in a real big building. It had lots of lights and people around. I tried to be as small as possible so no one would notice me, when suddenly I was airborne and a small voice squealed in my ear. A child (the little terror) had me in his clutches and was squeezing me so tight I couldn't breathe! Just as suddenly, this big lady grabbed me by my ear, and threw me in a big box and said that this little terror could not take things out of the box as they were gifts! I thought I was going to die!

There were some other things in the box with me. Some were really soft and others were cold and hard. There was a little white puppy in with me too. She told me we were going to be sent away and would be living with some children. When I thought of that little terror who had squeezed the breath out of me, I became afraid again. I wished I had never left the Travellers where I knew you would be coming back for me. How were you going to find me now? Would I ever see you again? I thought of all your friends and how they made me feel so special with trips and parties. (Yep, another photo of me between two boxes with red brick wrapping and sign that says "Toys for Tots.")

Almost in the Box

Through my tears, I watched as a hand reach into the box and lifted me out. What was going to happen now? I heard a lady say to her friend that she had heard on the radio that I was missing. They thought they had seen me thrown in the box, but now they didn't know what to do with me. As they walked along holding me (oh, it felt so good to be cuddled again), they discussed what to do with me. One of the ladies said maybe if they hung me on the Salvation Army kettle stand someone would recognize me and take me to where I belonged. (There is a picture of me hanging off the stand.)

Alas, that was not to be. Suddenly I was yanked off the stand and thrown into a car. I had been in cars before, so I thought maybe I was finally going home. After a while, they took me to a really fancy hotel. It was beautiful inside. I fell off the chair in the lobby where they put me and slipped behind a chair. I hear then looking for me but gave up real quick saying I was just a stuffed piece of junk anyways and their kids had nicer ones at home. I was so crushed!

When they left, I jumped up on the counter and tried to ask the pretty girls there if they could please phone you to come and get me, and to tell you that I was so sorry for all the trouble I had caused. I knew by now that you were so worried about me and had called the radio station to try and get me back. (Now there are two pictures in the hotel: one with two girls and one kicking me out.) For such a nice hotel, those young ladies were really rude. One grabbed me by my ear and kicked me right out the door!

Out in the snow I started to cry and thought that now I would never see you or the girls again. There was a good smell coming from across the street, so I decided I was hungry and maybe someone would give me something to eat over there. There were lots of people there, and I managed to scurry inside when the door opened. There were some men dressed in funny pants that reminded me of trees, which reminded me that I had to go real bad. Just as I squatted, one of these funny men picked me up and started to laugh at my purple body all covered with mud and snow. One of the men said they had heard on the radio that I was a mascot for the Red Hat Society in Peace River and that I was missing. Holding me tight, the men decided that I would make a good mascot for their group as they were heading out for Iraq! Mum!! THEY HAVE KIDNAPPED ME!

As a joke they have taken me with them. They say that I can be like that travelling gnome on TV and see the world. Mum, what do they mean? Please come and get me. They say I'll be lucky if I am home by January. They put me in this smelly bag called a duffle. There was some paper and a pencil. I am writing this note to let you know I am so sorry I ever left without telling you. If I can, I will try to get this note to you somehow. Just know, Mum, that I am safe so far, and I don't think they will hurt me. They say we are going to a party and it's called a war.

Till I see you again,

Sassy

(The last picture is of me with four army guys.)

Quite the letter, huh?!

I did not write that letter. Someone set me up and kept me hidden just to see what would happen. Rose said that after she got the letter, she read it out loud and watched the faces of the ladies for clues. She then put two and two together and figured out that this was a big hoax. As soon as she read "Mum," she knew. Her title is "Mascot Mum" not "MuM." She has a good idea who is doing it because of the computer-generated pictures. Nobody admits it though. She is not concerned about me anymore because I am really with one of the girls. No one is talking to Rose about who did this or why. Maybe whoever is doing it is sorry now but does not know what to do to fix the situation.

I have been doing a lot of thinking this past while. I think that the ladies were getting bored with taking me home, and I have lost my appeal with the group. The longer I am missing, the less people will care and want me to visit with them.

I have been remembering all the things I did last year. There was a reduation for Sue when she turned fifty; of course there are all those coffee nights at Travellers too; and I will never forget meeting the new mascot, Miss Scarlett O'Hatta, in Fairview; yep, I got another birthday party, cake and all; there was another reduation with a lot of teddy bears; that surprise birthday party for Rose where she works; I toured the Anglican Church; I was stuck in a tree and had a picture of me looking drunk with a glass of beer beside me; what a party for "Christmas in July" at Rose's place again; and saying goodbye to Jan was the hardest thing I had to do this year. I will sure miss her. The fiesta night at Sue's was sure a different party, as well at the surprise party for Judy and then there was the Festival of Trees again.

I wonder if I am missing any special functions. I know that there is coffee night twice a month that I am missing. Rose always has a Christmas party in December too. I remember that she said that she was going to have a chocolate fountain at the party. She was gave stockings to everyone back in July to decorate before being taken to the Salvation Army for kids for Christmas along with the yellow toys that everyone was buying. I heard that Rose found a cute little yellow teddy bear that would be from me.

I hear talking, and the conversation is about me again. They do not know what to do about me and this whole weird thing that has gotten totally out of control. They do not like Rose's not-worried attitude about me either. She keeps *insisting* that she is not worried about me anymore.

A normal mascot usually just sits in a person's home until a major function happens and then they might just attend and sit and watch the festivities. Maybe that is what will happen to me now. I think that maybe I should stay with Rose, and she can take me to coffee night and other parties. I know that she works full time and cannot attend everything, but when I do get a chance to go, it will be special for me and her.

I have not seen her in a long time and I am wondering how she is doing.

Again, I can hear voices. They are saying that it has been long enough, and it is time that I went back to Rose's place.

Someone is coming into the room. I can hear footsteps. I cannot see who it is. I got stuffed into a bag, carried out of the door and thrown onto the back seat of a vehicle. We drove real fast to Rose's place. There was no one home. The person took me out of the car and put me on Rose's sidewalk, took off the blindfold, turned around and just left me there. I sure hope it doesn't rain or a stray animal doesn't attack me.

I waited for a long time, just lying there, wondering what my life will be like now. It will not ever be like it used to be, that I know for sure. I love Rose, and she loves me, so for right now I guess that is all that matters.

I hear a vehicle pull up by the fence. Someone gets out. I hear the car door shut. The gate is opening. Thank goodness. IT'S ROSE! She just stopped and stared at me. Her eyes got real big. She walked over to me, stooped and picked me up, took me out of the bag and gave me a huge hug. I think there were tears in her eyes too. She took me into her place and sat me down on my little comfy chair.

"Welcome home!" she said. "You are just in time because I am planning a Red Hat Saint Patrick's Day party for tomorrow."

So, it is March 16 and I have been gone for almost four months!

I wonder what is going to happen now.

Chapter 9

Rose and I had a long talk about what has been happening since I have been gone. She said that she knows one person for sure who planned the fake kidnapping. I have done so much as a mascot, and this would be a big funny event. It got out of hand, and then no one really seemed to care about what was happening. Rose said that when she got the letter, she wanted to continue the story, "find" me on the side of the road and bring me home, but decided just to see what would happen next. Well, nothing happened for a long, long time. The longer I stayed away, the worse it got, and then everyone figured out that I was safe, and the girls just waited to see what would happen.

Rose had been keeping a storyline about me for a long time. When the kidnapping happened, she had to stop because the story was about the girls and me through my eyes, and I was not attending any functions or having fun. I was just stuck in a dark room all by myself. That little part of history will be gone now too. Yep, lots of changes are now happening with me and the Sassy REDs.

My life for sure will never be the same now. I am accepting that. I know that Rose will take me wherever we need to go. Maybe I will just be a "regular" mascot like all the rest of the mascots around the world. Or, maybe not …

Burt was sure surprised to see me when he got home. He smiled and said it was good to have me back and he was glad that I was not harmed in any way. I just smiled at him.

Rose is planning a Saint Patrick's Day party. She always does the Christmas in July, but this is special because her son, daughter-in-law and new granddaughter will be here too. Everyone is to bring something green for show and tell.

Happy St. Pat's Day everyone!

I sit in the kitchen and watch Rose make green food for the party. Looks like green cupcakes with green icing and shiny sprinkles. Here come all the ladies. Nancy, Rose's daughter-in-law, and Bailey, her granddaughter, are also attending this party. Rose introduced the ladies to Gem Trip, a green frog that Rose got the storytelling idea for me from. She also used Bailey who was dressed in green as her item for show and tell. Bailey cannot eat anything and has a special tube for feeding. She also has a trach to help her breathe. She is a very special granddaughter.

It sure feels good to attend a party again with all the girls. They all seem happy to have me back. I even got a few hugs.

Boy, this is a busy day. All the ladies left, and then Rose got busy again with a surprise party that same night for her husband. Some of the same people came back again. Burt was sure surprised to see everyone. He got a whole bunch of phone calls that evening too.

Edna was a good member for quite a while. When she went to see her doctor, she was told that she had real bad health problems. Rose told me that she died and went to heaven. Edna told a relative to contact the Sassy Reds to be an honour guard for her at her funeral. There were twenty-three ladies there for the funeral.

There is a *Guys and Dolls* play that the girls want to attend. There is that money thing again, so I cannot attend. I understand. I will just stay and watch TV with Burt.

It is April already. It is my birthday month. There is a new girl who has a birthday this month. With everything that has happened with me and the girls, I am not expecting any party or gifts this year. There is just not the same pizzazz that it had before the kidnapping.

Rose is still taking me to the coffee nights at Travellers. The girls are talking about finding a new place like the Senior's Centre to hold our coffee nights. Some of the girls are members. Our group is really quite large now too. No one is offering to take me home with them. Rose did not bring up the subject either. No one mentioned my birthday.

I have noticed that Rose is walking crooked lately.

"What's wrong Rose? You look like you are limping," I said.

"I am having problems with my shoulder," she said. "It is all the heavy lifting that I do at the bakery. I am going to see the doctor tomorrow. Would you like to come?"

"Is it okay for me to do that?" I asked.

"Why not? You have not been in a doctor's office before, haven't you?" she asked.

This sounds like another new adventure for me. The next day, Rose put my purple hat on me and away we went out the door to the car, buckled in and drove and parked at the building where all the doctors see their patients.

We got out of the vehicle and went into the building. Rose stopped at the front desk to check in, and then we sat down and waited to be called. There are sure a lot of people here and some of them are even smiling at me.

We finally walked to the office. The doctor looked at me kind of funny but still smiled. He asked Rose what was the idea of the "purple dog." That is what he called me. She giggled and then explained about me and the Sassy REDs and how I have fun with the girls. He giggled again and said that this has never happened to him but he understood.

He looked at Rose's shoulder and told her to take a couple of days off work. He gave her a note to give to her boss at the bakery. He also recommended that she get massages for the pain.

We left the office and then drove up to the bakery. Her boss was not there at the time so she left the note in his office for him to contact her. I stayed in the car until she got back, and then we went back home.

Rose was in such bad shape that again the doctor ordered her to take a lot of time off work. She stopped in at the bakery and explained what was happening and then we went back home. The lady that does the massages for Rose refused to do her back because there was a big lump on her shoulder. She's going to therapy at the hospital two times a week now too.

"Where are we going?" I asked Rose as she picked me up and carried me to the car.

"Another new place," was all that she said.

We drove up the big hill, past where she works and stopped at a huge building. We got out of the car, walked in the doors and went to the reception desk. Rose set me on the counter and talked to the lady. The lady smiled at me, and I smiled back. She did not ask who I was. Rose went to see the therapy specialist and made an appointment. He giggled when he saw me. I smiled at him. Rose explained who I was.

As we walked out of the building, Rose said that it was a hospital. People who are not well or need special care come here.

Rose is not doing the Christmas in July party at her place because she is not well enough with her bad shoulder.

Judy wants to hold the party at her place instead. It will be a "couples" barbecue. She has a nice big yard so everyone will be nice and comfortable. She has a nice fire pit too; they add logs to it and burn it for a couple of hours in the evenings. It sure was a fun get together with husbands.

I noticed that Rose is quite emotional at times. She said that she is thinking of quitting working at the bakery because of her shoulder. Her boss is already looking for someone to take her place. She has been off work for quite a while now, and the bakery really needs someone in her position. The therapy she has two times a week at the hospital is slowly helping.

"Hey, Rose, talk to me. What is happening?" I asked.

She said, "Well, lots right now. I start a new job on Tuesday. I will be working at a jewellery store. It is called B&C Jewellers. There are two sisters and one husband that own the business. The business was started by their father. He retired so the girls took it over."

Well, it is coffee night at Travellers again. The girls did a lot of talking about the Senior's Centre. We will be having our meetings there starting real soon. Everything has been arranged for us. There is lots of room for all the ladies that have joined our group.

Rose just told me that the Sassy REDs have been invited to a turkey supper in Grimshaw. She and I are getting a ride with

Judy for the evening. Judy picked us up, and I sat in the back seat and Rose sat in the front. We finally got to the building. It sure is a big place. We got out of the car and walked to the door and then stepped inside.

"Wow, look at this place," I said.

There were a lot of nice decorations. We sat down and ate turkey and all the rest of the trimmings. For dessert there was a variety of hats: a Valentine's hat, Saint Patrick's hat, Easter bonnet, and a Santa hat. What a unique idea. What a fun-filled evening.

Chapter 10

Well, it sure has been an interesting summer. Rose seems to be having fun at her new job. She is a real sales person so this is right up her alley. I wonder when she will take me there for a visit. I am sure that she has told the people working there about me and the Sassy REDs.

We are meeting at the Senior's Centre now. What a nice place. I do not have a special little chair, so I am sitting on the edge of the table. The girls move all the little tables into a big square or rectangle shape, and then everyone sits around the huge table. It sure works. There is a lot of room. The girls were saying that there is a pool table and other sports things downstairs that we can use to have fun.

Rose loves to play pool, so she said that she wants to have a coffee night turned into a pool night real soon.

Hmm, Rose has a real funny looking bright red spikey thing on her head. It almost looks like a Halloween wig but not quite. I wonder what she is up to now. She picked up a deck of cards and put them in her purse. I have not seen her do that before.

"What are you doing, Rose?"

She looked at me, smiled and said, "We are going to have fun tonight."

Rose put a cute little hat on my head, grabbed me and went out the door. We got buckled in the car and drove to the Senior's Centre for our meeting. After all the ladies got there, Rose said that we were all heading downstairs to play some pool. She said that it is a fun game and she would teach us how to play "poker pool."

We all went downstairs, and Rose dug out the deck of cards. She started to deal the cards into little piles. There were five cards for each of the ladies. She set up the pool balls on the table, grabbed a pool cue, aimed and did the shot. The balls went all over the table. She explained that the numbers on the cards match the numbers on the balls. It does not matter who sinks any given ball. If anyone has the same card as the sunken ball, it counts. The first person to get rid of all their cards wins the game. There is no real contest, and it is a fun way to play pool. The girls loved the game so much that they played two games.

When the second game was over, everyone went home. That sure was a fun time. It was something new for the girls.

Rose was talking to me about a Red Hat jewellery party that she is thinking of attending. She used to sell jewellery when she lived in British Columbia. It is the same company.

Well, it finally time for the jewellery party. Rose wears a nice red hat and she put my casual hat on me. We got in the car, buckled up and away we went. We parked, got out of the car and walked to Debbie's house.

There are a bunch of ladies here. The sales lady explained about the jewellery. One of the ladies volunteered to model the items to let everyone see what it looks like when someone is wearing it. There is sure a big variety of necklaces, bracelets, earrings and other things.

Rose works in a jewellery store now, so she knows about the quality of the items. The sales lady was quite surprised. There was a snack after the demonstration.

Well, it is just about time for Orange Night again. Reva is planning the party tonight. All the girls were asked to bring a baby picture and a current picture so the ladies can try and figure out what the girls looked like way back then. It was a fun game.

There were a bunch of baby pumpkins too. The girls were given one and had to carve a special face on it. The girls got to take them home with them.

For another game, we had to identify different candy. Reva had cut different little candy bars and gave them a number. She also had all the names of the bars. We all had to try to guess what bar went with what number. It was a great evening. It is so nice to be attending parties again.

There were special sandwiches to eat and orange juice for a drink.

It sure is getting cold and snowy outside again. Rose will be planning her Christmas party soon.

At the last coffee night, the girls decided that they do not want to attend the Festival of Trees or put in an entry this year. It is a lot of work, and the girls do not want to get involved. The prices to get in to the gala event have changed, and there have been other changes too.

The girls are talking about having supper at the Senior's Centre instead of the regular Christmas party that Rose usually has at her place. The Senior's Centre group have a turkey/ham meal every year. Everyone liked the idea, so that is what will happen this year. Rose decided that she will not be going because she will still be working when the supper is on.

I heard later that it was a great meal and there was a great turnout.

Ooh, it sure is cold outside. It is thirty-seven degrees below zero. Good weather to just stay home and keep warm.

Because the girls went out for supper and Rose did not have her party, Sue decided to have a Red Hat get together at her place. I did not get to go because Rose was working that day and the party was in the afternoon. We heard later that it was a great party.

Well, Christmas is over, so that means the end of the year is close too. What a year it has been again.

The girls are sure enjoying having their meetings at the Senior's Centre. They are talking about doing an arts and crafts night, a valentine's party and a second-hand clothing sale.

Rose is busy making some sort of special food. I wonder if we are going somewhere special. It looks like food to take to a pot luck supper. I have been to those parties before.

"Do you want to go for supper?" Rose asked.

"I would love to," I replied.

She put a special hat on my head, put on her coat and boots, picked up the food and then we both got in the car and away we went to the Senior's Centre. Wow, there are sure a lot of ladies here. It is a good thing we are meeting here now.

"Happy new year, everyone!" I exclaimed.

Everyone was wishing everyone else a happy new year. After everyone ate, we just sat and chatted about all we did for the holidays. We also discussed having a valentine's party. Everyone liked that idea.

Rose and I went back home, and I sat on my special chair. It is nice and high so that Casper the cat has not attacked or even threatened me in any way.

"Hey, Sassy, it is time to go out again. The girls are going to have fun tonight," Rose said.

We drove back to the Senior's Centre. It was all decorated with red and white hearts. There sure are a lot of ladies here.

Everyone was giggling and working on valentine's cards. It was sure a special evening.

Not much has happened except for coffees lately.

Rose is hauling out suitcases. I wonder what she is up to now. She and Burt were talking about visiting relatives in Creston, British Columbia. I wonder where that is. It sounds like it is a long ways away.

"Hey, Rose, are you planning a trip somewhere?" I finally asked her.

"Yes, we are. Burt and I have been planning this for a while now."

"Am I going to stay here all by myself, or am I going to stay with some Red Hat ladies while you are gone?"

"Well," she said, "I think I will take you with us."

"Me, go on holiday with you? What a great idea!" I replied.

I started to get real excited. I have gone on little day trips, but this will be a lot of travelling and seeing new places and people.

"When are we leaving?" I asked excitedly.

"In a couple of days," she answered.

I was so excited. Finally, the day came. Rose and Burt packed all the suitcases in the car and then Rose finally picked me up and put me on the back seat and buckled me in. Her husband commented about it, but she just giggled and said that Sassy would not like being in the back seat without the belt on.

Boy, we sure travelled for a long ways. Pretty soon we stopped at a little town, and Burt and Rose went into a little motel and booked it for the night. They hauled in their suitcases and then came and got me. It is a long trip, and it is too long to try and do all in one day.

The next morning, they got dressed and then loaded the suitcases and put them back in the car and buckled me in. We drove a long way again, and then we stopped at a café. I cannot see the name of it from the back seat. Burt and Rose left me in the car while they went in for breakfast.

Soon we were back on the road again. Burt and Rose have travelled this road quite a few times.

"Hey, Sassy, look up there," Rose pointed. "Those are mountains. They will get bigger as we travel farther into British Columbia."

"Wow, some of them are sure big and there is snow on them too," I said.

"Those are glaciers," she answered.

The road sure got narrower and is winding with lots of corners now. What an adventure. We travelled through a lot of towns and cities. What a difference from Peace River country.

We stopped several times because they had to get gasoline for the car and munchies for snacking.

We finally got to the town called Creston. It was in this area that Burt and Rose lived before moving to Peace River. We found a motel, and they booked the room for several days.

Burt and Rose unloaded the car and then brought me in and set me on a special little chair. I am so tired. I think I will take a little nap.

Winding roads, big mountains, lots of trees, white flowing water and bumps on the road. I woke up. I was having another dream.

I hear music that sounds like a marching band going by, and I can see beautiful decorated vehicles, clowns, horses and lots of other things.

Burt and Rose got back and explained that this is a special weekend in Creston. It is a festival called the Blossom Festival, which is held on the long weekend in May every year. Burt and Rose were involved with this organization for a lot of years as executives. There are lots of things happening all weekend. I have to stay in the motel because there is so much going on that I may get stolen or lost. Yep, after my kidnapping scare, I agreed with them. I will just wait for them right here.

Burt and Rose have come and gone quite a few times in the past couple of days. They sure look excited when they get back to the motel.

A few days later, they tell me that their visit is now over and we are heading to the Okanagan. That is a large area where a lot of fruit is grown. They said that they have a friend that they want to visit in that area.

They packed up their suitcases and put me on the back seat again, buckled me in and away we went. We travelled down this real winding, narrow road for a long time and then we stopped. I saw a huge bunch of water. Rose told me that it is called Kootenay Lake. We are waiting for a huge ferry to take us across the lake.

Here comes the ferry. It is called the Osprey. There is no charge to get on this ferry. We all waited in the car until the ferry ride was done. We drove off the ferry and were back on narrow winding roads again. We stopped a couple of times for gas and food. The mountains are smaller here than what we saw earlier. We drove through a bunch more towns again. We finally stopped at a trailer in a little town called Tappen.

"Well, Sassy, we are finally here to visit this special friend," Rose said.

She unbuckled me, and the three of us went to the trailer and rang the doorbell.

The door opened.

"JAN!!!" I screamed. "Oh, Jan! It is *so* good to see you again after all this time!"

"Sassy! Oh, Sassy! I missed you too!" Jan exclaimed.

We went into Jan's home. There were hugs all around. What a surprise! We had a great time talking about all that has happened with the Sassy REDs. Jan is involved with a group of girls here. They are having a meeting tomorrow. Jan wants me and Rose to come to the meeting to meet everyone. Jan set me on a special little comfy chair. Boy, I sure am tired. I think I will take a nap.

"Good night, girls." I said. I closed my eyes.

Real deep water, a big ferry, a big high mountain, winding roads, big rain drops on the windshield, lots of cars and trucks, so many new things I have never seen before …

I felt someone shaking me. I opened my eyes. What a dream again. There was Jan waking me up.

"I want you to attend a Red Hat party this afternoon," she said.

"I would love to," I replied.

Rose, Jan and I went to a big building. We walked in and sat with a bunch of Red Hat ladies. Jan introduced me to them. They looked at me kind of funny. They were wondering why a mascot would travel so far for no real reason. Well, I am a unique mascot and always have been. Jan and Rose were telling the ladies some of the things that have happened to me. They looked real funny at me again. Yeah, I understand that most mascots just sit and wait for a major event to happen, but I have been different right from day one.

It was a great afternoon. We got back home and I got to sit on that comfy chair. The folks went to town and to some stores.

We spent a couple of days with Jan and Heinz. Here we go again, packing up the suitcases. We all hugged goodbye and then back into the car and on the road again. This is a different way home. There is all new scenery again. We made our usual stops for gas and food. I stayed in the back seat. I even napped a couple of times. It is very hard just sitting in a vehicle for long periods of time.

Finally, we are back in Peace River. What a vacation.

CHAPTER 11

I was watching Rose. It looked like she had a big red funny looking piece of clothing with two big bumps on it. She just bought it and was taking it out of the shopping bag.

"What is that?' I asked.

She giggled and then said, "It is a red bra. Women wear this piece of clothing on their chests under their regular clothes."

"Oh."

"Yes, we are having a special coffee tonight. We are going to make bra hats and bra purses."

"Oh, can I come?"

"Sure, let's go," she said.

We got in the car and drove to the Senior's Centre. The girls already had the tables set up and everyone brought different beads, flowers, hot glue guns, ribbon and a variety of other fun things. The girls sure were doing a lot of giggling. There was sure a variety of bras. The ladies took scissors and cut the ends off and the straps and then started to glue things together. Most of the girls put the hats on their heads and then went to the bathroom to see how they looked.

We all agreed that we will have to have a special outing and all of us will wear the hats.

Well, Ellen wants to have her annual pot luck supper at her place again. I have been there before. She has a large house and acreage.

Rose is planning to go, and she is preparing a cold platter. She put a special hat on me, and we jumped in the car, put on seatbelts and drove to Ellen's place. Wow. Look at all the ladies here for this fun time. Let me count. There are twenty-four.

We all enjoyed the meal and discussed what we will do next. The girls mentioned that Fia is visiting again from Norway and has relatives that own a Saskatoon berry farm.

"Hey, Rose, what are Saskatoon berries?"

"They are little purple berries that grow on bushes. They are great to eat and make great pies and cupcakes," she answered.

The girls decided that going there will be our next outing because the berries will be ripe by then. We also decided that we will all wear our bra hats. We will even bring one for Fia to wear.

Time really has gone quickly. It is now time to go to the Saskatoon berry farm. Judy picked up me and Rose. Boy, it is a long drive. Finally, we got there. A lot of ladies are here too. We were introduced to the owners of the farm. Fia sure did giggle when she saw all the bra hats and figured out what they were originally. There was a big huge machine that went up and down the rows of trees and picked the berries. Most of the ladies remembered picking the berries with they were younger. We all got fresh berries to eat. What a treat!

Well, another coffee night. Usually the girls have something planned now because we have the time and space to do things other than just drinking coffee. Nope, looks just like coffee and talking tonight.

Judy wants to have a barbecue again for husbands too. They are really fun.

Where has the summer gone? It is getting cool, the leaves are mostly gone off the trees, and I have even seen a couple of flakes of snow.

The coffee meetings have been fun as usual. It is time for orange night again. Rona is hosting the event.

Rose put my special Halloween hat on me. She has an orange boa on her head instead of a hat. It has a black spider on it too. We drove to the house. There were decorations on the door. The house was all decorated with ghosts, spiders, witches and skulls. These are real nice Halloween decorations. There are fourteen ladies here, which is a good turnout.

It was a good time.

Rose has been at the jewellery store for quite a while now. It is a place that she really enjoys working at.

"Hey, Sassy," Rose said. "The girls at work want to meet you. They know that I am really involved with the Sassy REDs."

"Today?" I asked.

"Yes, it is Thursday and everyone comes in today. The store is open late like a lot of the stores in Peace River. I told everyone about you, but telling people what you look like and really seeing you are two different things."

"It sounds like fun. How about if I wear my boa? It sounds like it will be a special visit," I said.

"Of course."

Rose went and found me a special hat and my little red boa. She put them on me. I felt real special. We got in the car and drove to where she works. We parked in the back lot and walked into the back door. Rose sat me on the little table that the workers use for their coffee and lunch breaks.

I was introduced to all of the staff. There were the two owners. Lynne does the repairs and Bev does the purchasing. Lynne's husband was there too. His name is Peter, and he does all the engraving. There were also a few other girls who work there. I said hi to everyone and smiled at them. They loved my eyes. I sure got lots of hugs from everyone. I peeked around the corner a few times and watched Lynne repair necklaces and change batteries in watches. The girls are sure busy cleaning the shelves and looking after customers. What a learning day.

Another coffee night. The girls are talking about a special event. It is called Crimson and Ice. It will be a special vegetarian meal and we will have a guest speaker. There will be a charge, so I will not be attending. There are quite a few of the girls who are planning to attend.

Well, it is close to Christmas again. Rose has decided that this will be her final Christmas party. It will be held at the Senior's Centre because our group is so big and everyone is used to being at the centre now.

Rose and I arrived and were surprised that there were twenty-one ladies present. What a great turnout. This has been her tenth party in five years. She says that it is time for the group as a whole to plan parties this big and not just for one person. Rose is doing the "unwrap the box" game again. The ladies loved that game. Everyone brought their decorated stocking, which will be donated to the Salvation Army for kids for Christmas. Someone thought up a question and answer game. We even had a gift exchange.

Well, Christmas is over, that means New Year's is just around the corner. There are lots of ladies here for the coffee chat. The girls are talking about plans for the next couple of months. Things like a movie night, a special tea, a supper and a clothing exchange.

At the next coffee night, Martha said that she wants to show a movie at her home the following week. It will be Sue's sixty-second birthday too. The movie was *Grease*. What a great movie.

Well it is tea, not coffee, time. There is a good turnout of ladies here. We played a little game that was called "remember your childhood." Each girl had to tell a story that happened when they were young. There were sure lots of different stories.

It is that time of the year for the annual musical at the Peace Players. The girls always go to TJ's for a meal and then go to the play. Usually ladies from Falher are there too. The play this year is called *Camelot*.

The girls are having a clothes exchange. Everyone is to bring some good clothes that they do not wear anymore and we will all swap clothes. Anything left over with be donated to a second hand clothing store in Grande Prairie.

Burt had a long talk with me the other day. Rose will be sixty real soon. Their son and his wife have been making phone calls and sending e-mail and are planning a surprise party for her in the park after she gets off work. Burt has been running around finding tables and chairs and moving the barbecue. Rose is working today and has no clue what is happening. Burt took me out to the park before Rose got home. He said that he was going to lie to her and tell her that he found something at a yard sale that he wanted her to look at and then decide if they wanted to buy it. Sounds like a plan to me.

Here they come. He is stopping the car, and they are both getting out. Look at her. She looks so surprised. There are a whole bunch of Red Hat and other ladies here including her son, Jason, daughter-in-law, Nancy, and granddaughter, Bailey.

Yep, we all pulled it off just great. There was even a huge birthday cake for her. She sure is excited. Everyone sang "Happy Birthday" to her. We all left to go home a couple of hours later.

CHAPTER 12

The girls and I have been to a lot of different eateries in Peace River. Rose told me that we are going to a new place today for brunch. The restaurant has not been opened very long. Burt and Rose have been here for special occasions for supper.

She put a hat on me, picked me up and away we went again, buckled up in the car. We got to the restaurant and walked in. Boy, there sure are a lot of ladies here. Brunch was sure good. I got to sit in a little chair again.

The girls are talking about an invitation to attend an Olympic event with the girls at Grimshaw.

"Hey, girls, what is an Olympic event?" I asked.

"It is fun and games and you win medals for first, second and third place," someone said.

"It sure sounds like fun. Can I come too?"

"Of course," said about six ladies all together.

The girls were also talking about having that clothing sale and fashion show. We can hold that at the Senior's Centre at the next coffee chat.

See you all soon, ladies.

Finally it is time to go to Grimshaw. I have really been looking forward to this event. Rose has a bit of a sore leg. She seems to be limping a little. I sure hope that she does not have trouble at the Olympics.

Judy said that she will pick me and Rose up and drive to the event. We finally got to the hall where the event was being held. There sure are a lot of ladies here. There are a lot of different things on the floor for the different races. The girls are having fun jumping up and down and running races all over the place. Someone keeps track of the races and the winners. At the end, the winners were presented with gold, silver and bronze medals.

"Me?" Someone called my name, and I said, "Me?"

My Gold Medal!

Someone said, "Yes, you, Sassy. Thank you for coming to this event. Here is a medal for you." She put one around my neck. I felt so proud to get a medal. We all said goodbye, and then Judy drove me and Rose home. I will wait now for the fashion show.

"Let's go, Sassy," Rose said. On went my hat again and away we went to the car and then to the Senior's Centre. Again, there is a good turnout of ladies. There are sure a lot of clothes. The girls were real busy running into the bathroom to try clothes on to see it they would fit them. The clothes that were left over would be donated to a thrift store.

Well, it is orange night again. This sure seems to be a popular event for the girls. I got to wear my orange hat again. There was a gift exchange and everyone drew numbers. What a great number of prizes. Everyone was pleased with the gifts that they got to take home. After all the coffee cups were washed, we went home.

Burt and Rose are having that special supper again. She has been cooking the turkey all day. It sure smells good. There are a lot of people here again for this special day with their religion.

Oh no. Something is wrong. Burt went into the laundry room and saw water sitting on the floor. He moved a couple of things and there was more water. He ripped up some of the flooring and found black mold under the flooring on the wood. This is not good. They may have to rip up everything and have to fix the floor. They do not know how much damage there is. The next day, they contacted their insurance company. They had some guys here during the day to see what was happening. They were told that they have to leave and move into a motel for a few days and that they are not allowed back in the trailer. I see them packing a suitcase and heading out the door.

They forgot all about me. I will okay here. Casper, the cat, is still here too. They are back now. The room has got plastic on the door so they cannot get into the bedroom now. They did a quick walk through and then went back out again.

Some guys brought in big machines to dry the floor. Now they are moving things around and packing a bunch of stuff in boxes. I sure hope that I do not end up in the bottom of a box. They are not labelling the boxes. How will Burt and Rose know what is in each box?

It has been a couple of days. Burt and Rose are back. They are picking up more things and grabbed me and Casper.

"Where are we going? I asked.

"We have bad water damage. They will be ripping out the walls, washer and dryer, flooring, toilet, bathtub, and even all the cupboards," Rose said. We have to move into a motel for a while, so we may as well have you with us."

"Oh no," I exclaimed.

We got to the motel. It was a little kitchenette room with one bed and two chairs, a little fridge, cupboard and stove. Casper was sure fidgety and tried to hide under the bed.

Rose and Burt still went to work each day. The motel was close to where they both work. They sure were talking a lot about how much time it was taking to get things done. Only one or two men would show up and work for a few hours, and then nothing would happen for a few days. It was early in the morning and I heard a funny noise. It sounded like a snapping sound. It is real cold outside. Suddenly water started to run down the walls from the roof.

Burt and Rose really looked and saw the water on the walls and then on the floor. This is not good. They phoned down to the office and were told that someone upstairs right above them left the water running and one of the pipes broke, causing the water to run down the walls. We were told to quickly pack everything and get out of the room. Boy, did we ever do that quickly. We were then set up in another room. Burt grabbed Casper, Rose grabbed me and away we went to another room. What a story to tell the staff at work!

The company is still taking a long time to do the work. They only work for an hour or so and then they are off for a few days. These guys do not really seem to care. They are leaving big globs of cement on the floor, cigarette butts on the table and dirt all over.

Burt and Rose are getting concerned about how long it is taking and whether they will be able to be home for Christmas or if they will still be in the motel. It is very expensive on a weekly basis.

Burt went out and bought a little green Christmas tree to surprise Rose. She was so happy.

Nope, they will not be back in the trailer until maybe sometime in January. They went to see their son and his family in Grande Prairie for the Christmas holiday. Casper was having a real hard time, so they took him back to the trailer because he was less stressed out there. It was just me and the cute little tree for Christmas.

It is the middle of January and things are still slow at the trailer. The sewage lines froze because the guys left the little door open under the trailer. There is sure a lot of stress with Burt and Rose having to go through this. They contacted the company who was responsible for the work and told them that they could not afford to stay in the motel anymore. They just did not have any more money. The company would not do anything.

Then a miracle happened. Joyce and her husband said that they were going away in January until March and asked Burt and Rose to stay at their place and look after it for them. What a great idea. Burt and Rose moved into Joyce's place. They left Casper at home but took me with them to stay at the house.

Well, the floor is now in and the cupboards are here. Burt and Rose had to supply the knobs for the cupboards. It sure has been stressful. I sure hope that we can move back into the trailer real soon.

Now it is the end of January and things are still moving slowly. Burt and Rose had to supply a new toilet and bathtub for the bathroom and a new kitchen sink. They got the kitchen rewired and a new dishwasher while everything was ripped out. The painter finally painted the walls.

It is now February and things are finally getting done. Everything seems to be getting back to where it should be. By Valentine's Day, Burt and Rose were told they could move back in! It has been three long months to do a job that should not have taken this long. Burt and Rose are waiting for a cleaning crew to come in and do the cleaning. No one showed up, so Burt and Rose had to do it themselves. What a nightmare for all of us. On the positive side, they have a beautiful trailer now. It is so good to be back here instead of in a motel room and someone else's home.

I wonder what will happen now.

Chapter 13

Rose told me that Joyce will be sixty-five in a couple of days. She will be a legal senior citizen by Canadian standards. That is an important birthday year.

Well, it is coffee time again at the Senior's Centre. There are sure a lot of ladies here. Someone baked a birthday cake for Joyce and everyone sang "Happy Birthday" to her. I remember what that was like once upon a time.

Rose is really enjoying working at the jewellery store. The owners and other girls have been taking about the Sassy Reds again and want me to visit with them again. Rose talked to me about it and I agreed. I had a lot of fun last time.

She put a special hat on me and then packed her huge beautiful purple hat with a bunch of flowers on it. It is her birthday hat that she wears in the month of May.

Rose unlocked the back door and we walked in. She sat me on the little table that the workers sit at for their breaks. Rose took out the big hat from the white plastic bag and set it beside me.

Peter came in and said hi to me. I smiled back at him. One of the girls put on the hat. It looked gorgeous on her. Peter even took a couple of pictures. I really enjoyed being in the store. The owners are such great people. Rose has talked a lot to them about the Sassy REDs, but they are not interested in joining. They figure that the girls are a little "out there."

Rose is talking to Judy on the phone. I can only hear her side of the conversation, and it does not sound good. After she hung up, Rose told me that Judy and her husband have sold their property and are planning to move real soon.

Thoughts flashed back to when Jan moved. That is when Judy became the queen. We will need a new queen again. I wonder who it will be next. There are so many talented ladies that would be great queens. Of course some of the ladies would not be interested at all.

The girls are talking about having a goodbye party for Judy. That sounds like a great idea. She and Jan were the two ladies who started this group and now both of them will not be living in Peace River any more.

"What are you doing, Rose?" I asked.

"Well, Sue always thought that Peg and I could do a Sonny and Cher song called "I Got You Babe," so I am practicing my moves," she said.

Rose found the song and then recorded it on a tape and kept playing and practising the lyrics. Peg even came over to rehearse. Rose is going to wear her special purple dress. Sue has a long black wig and a great big fake diamond ring for her to wear.

Well, it is finally the goodbye party for Judy. Again there is a good crowd of ladies. There were a bunch of different acts, including the one with Rose and Peg singing that song.

This will be the last coffee with Judy for a while since she is moving to Lloydminster. A lot of the talk that night was about Judy moving.

The girls are now talking about a special coronation for our new queen. Queen Sue. A couple of the girls contacted Rose and said that they found a stuffed purple gorilla that they want Sue to have for a mascot. In order for that to happen, I would have to resign as the reigning mascot. The girls said that each new queen from now on will have their own special mascot.

Queen Sue

When Rose found out about this, she was very sad and hurt. I talked to her and said that everything would be just fine. I could retire and stay with her like I have been for the past couple of years.

Rose and I talked a lot about my life since she found me at the yard sale, oh, so long ago. I told her that it would be nice if I passed the torch to the new mascot. The gorilla was a boy not a girl! Rose made him a black top hat and cane that I could pass to him as the new mascot. Rose even wrote up a goodbye speech for me.

It is finally Sue's coronation. There are ladies here from Falher, Grimshaw and Fairview again. There is that sea of red and purple that I am really going to miss.

Rose put the cape on Sue. Now it is my turn. Rose held me and read my goodbye speech. I talked about some of the funny things that happened to me, like being stuffed in the trunk of the car, having my head stuck out of a sun roof, celebrating my birthdays, falling in love, travelling to other towns and, of course, visiting the girls. Everyone giggled and then clapped at the end of the speech.

Ah, yes. Retirement. What will I be doing now? Rose and I drove home and she sat me on my favourite little chair. It is now my permanent place.

Oh, I am so sad that this has happened.

Now I guess I am officially retired. No more meetings, just sitting and watching Rose and her husband do their thing.

What is happening! It is summer of 2012. Something is going on! Why are there boxes all over the place? I guess I will find out soon. Wow, there is a big truck in the yard. Most of the furniture and a lot of boxes are going in the truck. I guess we are moving to a new town.

Burt is no longer here. Now Rose is gone for a couple of days.

It will not be long now for me to see where I will be living. Burt is back and they have loaded the car and the truck with things, including the grey cat that keeps looking at me kind of funny at times. I am sitting on the front seat with the seat belt on me. Boy, this is a long trip. It took four hours.

Hey, we're in a nice little basement suite in a town called Westlock. Burt is working at Home Hardware here. Rose is going to work for a while and then she decided that she just wants to retire. She is old enough to do that.

Here we go again. There are a whole bunch of boxes being packed. We are moving to a big house. No pets allowed. The grey cat got sick and was put to sleep. I do not have to worry about being attacked any more.

Burt and Rose are involved with the community. They both served on the Centennial Committee for two years. They had lots of mini meetings here. The mayor even showed up for a meeting.

There are Red Hatters in Westlock. Yep, they contacted Rose to join. There are two groups, but they are both not registered. That seems to frustrate Rose because the Sassy REDs were a legitimate group. Later, another group was started in the area that was registered.

I met a bunch of the Red Hat ladies for lunch. Rose introduced me to them. Hhhhmmmmm, Rose is not going to join the Scarlet Runners. I totally understand. She is involved with the Friends of the Library now, so she is quite busy. They are a group that does fundraising for the library. She was their treasurer for two years and now is president for two years too.

Rose put me in the window so I could see what is happening outside. The only bad thing is that I am two colours now! Light purple on the front and darker purple on my back. The sun faded me! Rose finally realized it and moved me.

Hey, here we go again. Boxes, boxes, boxes. She even put me in a big box with my other friends. Kind of cramped, but we all fit. No breathing problems.

Burt and Rose bought themselves a trailer on property in Westlock. I guess that means I will be here for a long time. They have lived here for almost five years now. Where has the time gone?

Wow. Sharon dropped in. I do not know if she saw me, but I saw her. There is a fifteen year reunion of the Sassy REDs in Peace River. It would be great to see those ladies again. I hear Rose making arrangements to go. Sounds like it will be a fun time. I am looking forward to seeing the mascot they have now.

I remember some fun times I had:

- Sitting in a high chair at meetings so I could see everyone
- Being put in the trunk of a car on a trip

- Travelling to other towns
- Meeting new members
- Attending special parties
- Visiting members' homes
- Sticking my head out of the top of a car window
- Watching a moon eclipse
- Going to the Festival of Trees
- And, of course, being kidnapped

I am so excited to be back in Peace River for this fifteen year reunion. Rose and I are staying at Sharon's place. She went with Sharon to help decorate the hall. When she came back, she was so excited.

The Sassy Reds have a new queen again. Queen Betty.

Queen Betty

Rose helped me write a thank you to all the girls and let them know what has happened in my life since retiring, oh, so long ago.

When it was Rose's turn to talk, she thanked the ladies for the invite. She read my story and then asked if any of the Sassy Reds would like to adopt me. One lady quickly raised her hand and said, "Yes, I would love to adopt Sassy!"

Rose walked over to this lady and said, "Here you go. Sassy is now yours." This lady is a member of the Red Hat Society in Grimshaw.

I smiled at her. She gave me a big hug and said that she loved me.

She made me feel so good.

…lved with the Red Hat
…n.
…ow.

…ne time gone? I remember so
… that yard sale table when this
…d me …

About the Author

In 2002, while living in Peace River, Alberta, Rose Olson became a member of the Sassy REDs, a registered group of the Red Hat Society.

In 1997, she self-published a book: Kitchener the History and the Memories. It is the one hundred year history of that small community in British Columbia.

She now lives in Westlock, Alberta.

CPSIA information can be obtained
at www.ICGtesting.com
Printed in the USA
LVHW052048280219
609134LV00004B/7

9 780228 807261